PRAISE FOR *TURNAROUND GOD*

"Our communities need to see a demonstration of God's turnaround power. It is our role as His church to be those who take His light into the darkness; lead the broken to wholeness. This book will challenge and inspire as it paints a picture of the limitless nature of our turnaround God and our access as believers to that incredible power."

—DARLENE ZSCHECH

"If there is one thing I know it's that God can turn around any situation. Nothing is too difficult for God. What is impossible for man is possible for God. You will be inspired by Charlotte's story and challenged to believe God can turn things around in your own life."

—CHRISTINE CAINE
FOUNDER, THE A21 CAMPAIGN
BEST-SELLING AUTHOR OF *UNDAUNTED*

"I have known Charlotte and her family for some years. Our lives collided in the late '90s and as with all collisions of destiny we have watched her life and ministry increase and bless many. Charlotte is a truly gifted communicator with a genuine heart for people. As she shares from her experience of both life and 'love affair with God', I am confident that this book *Turnaround God* will enlarg͏͏ eart and world."

—BOBBIE HOUSTON
ᴴILLSONG CHURCH
AUSTRALIA

"Charlotte Gambᴸ ͏ ᴜ awaken all of us who are simply coasting ͏ ͏t to live an ordinary life with God as a side dish tᴸ ͏s book up. In *Turnaround God* you will be reminded anew ͏wer and purpose of our Great God. It's refreshingly inspirationaͺ ͏ͺd challenging all at the same time."

—PETE WILSON
PASTOR, CROSS POINT CHURCH
AUTHOR OF *PLAN B* AND *LET HOPE IN*

"Charlotte's teaching and writing has had a profound impact on my life. She helps the truths of the Bible leap off the page and find a place in my everyday life. *Turnaround God* will be a lifeline to so many, including me, helping us to wholeheartedly believe in the power of the Living God who can turn anything and everything around."

—NATALIE GRANT
GOSPEL MUSIC'S 5-TIME FEMALE ARTIST OF THE YEAR
GRAMMY-NOMINATED RECORDING ARTIST

"In *Turnaround God* Charlotte challenges each of us to see things the way God does so we can, in turn, see His actions on our behalf. As you turn these pages you will capture God's vantage and receive His challenge to live beyond the possible!"

—LISA BEVERE
AUTHOR AND SPEAKER
MESSENGER INTERNATIONAL

"I love Char Gambill's heart for God and His people. She moves us from looking at God through the window of our experiences to looking at our lives through the window of the heart of God. That small shift changes everything!"

—SHEILA WALSH
WOF SPEAKER
AUTHOR OF *GOD LOVES BROKEN PEOPLE*

"I first met Charlotte in 1999 and immediately knew that she was destined to have global impact on the Body of Christ. Since then, she has traveled to the nations of the world telling thousands upon thousands about God's ability to transform any situation. Charlotte is a close friend of mine, and I have seen firsthand this important truth working in her own life on so many levels. She is living proof of God's ability to turn around any situation, no matter how impossible it may seem. This book will undoubtedly build your faith to believe that God's turnaround power is available to you."

—NANCY ALCORN
FOUNDER AND PRESIDENT, MERCY MINISTRIES
AUTHOR OF *MISSION OF MERCY*

"If you want to change directions, see things turned around in your life, or turn toward a better tomorrow you have found the right book. You will learn the principles of how to have a turnaround and receive what you hoped your life would be."

—JENTEZEN FRANKLIN
SENIOR PASTOR, FREE CHAPEL
NEW YORK TIMES BEST-SELLING AUTHOR OF *FASTING*

"Charlotte has truly captured the transforming power of God in her new book *Turnaround God*. This is the best of Charlotte and an absolute must-read for *every* believer! You will not only grow in your personal walk with God, but you will learn how you can live a victorious life through the power of our redemptive God. Taken on a journey of personal stories, riveting illustrations, and meaningful scripture, you will not be able to put this book down!"

—WENDY TREAT
SENIOR PASTOR, CHRISTIAN FAITH CENTER
SEATTLE, WASHINGTON

"*Turnaround God* is a thought-provoking read that celebrates God's power to overcome any circumstance. It is far too easy to give in to self-doubt and depression, but we are made to be conquerors in Jesus' name. There is no need to embrace defeat, for we serve a God of miraculous transformational power. This book is a call to action for the body of Christ, urging us to thrive in the calling on our lives. Charlotte Gambill writes with enthusiasm, compassion, and a deep understanding of the Word of God that makes each chapter come to life. For anyone who is wondering when a breakthrough will come or looking for a new spark in life, I would highly recommend this book. *Turnaround God* is a celebration of the victory that comes from following Christ, and it is sure to give readers a deeper understanding of their walk with God."

—PASTOR MATTHEW BARNETT
COFOUNDER, THE DREAM CENTER

TURNAROUND
GOD

TURNAROUND
GOD

Discovering God's
Transformational Power

CHARLOTTE GAMBILL

W Publishing Group

An Imprint of Thomas Nelson

Published in Nashville, Tennessee, by W Publishing Group. W Publishing Group is a registered trademark of Thomas Nelson, Inc.

Thomas Nelson, Inc., titles may be purchased in bulk for educational, business, fund-raising, or sales promotional use. For information, please e-mail SpecialMarkets@ThomasNelson.com.

Unless otherwise noted, Scripture quotations are taken from the Holy Bible, New International Version®. Copyright © 1973, 1978, 1984, 2011 by Biblica, Inc.™ Used by permission of Zondervan. All rights reserved worldwide. www.zondervan.com

Scripture quotations marked MSG are taken from *The Message* by Eugene H. Peterson. © 1993, 1994, 1995, 1996, 2000. Used by permission of NavPress Publishing Group. All rights reserved.

Scripture quotations marked NLT are taken from the *Holy Bible*, New Living Translation. © 1996. Used by permission of Tyndale House Publishers, Inc., Wheaton, Illinois 60189. All rights reserved.

Library of Congress Cataloging-in-Publication Data Available Upon Request

ISBN 978-0-8499-2189-6

Printed in the United States of America

13 14 15 16 17 RRD 6 5 4 3 2 1

CONTENTS

1. Time for Things to Turn?   1

2. Take Your Turn   19

3. Sticking Points   35

4. Turn the Other Cheek   55

5. Maturity Matters   73

6. Own Your Zone   93

7. A Permanent Investment   113

8. Unlikely Candidate   129

9. Not Qualified   145

10. Removing Restrictions   165

11. Personal Involvement   185

12. Turning It Over   203

Acknowledgments   225

ONE

TIME FOR THINGS TO TURN?

"SO WHAT DO YOU THINK?" CAME THE QUESTION FROM MY pregnant friend and her husband as we stood together on a wet, bleak hill in the English countryside. Shivering and trying to avoid being blown away by the relentless, gale-force winds, my husband and I took in the full scale of the project our friends were embarking upon. In front of us was an old, tumbledown barn with a sagging roof, rotting wooden doors, and no windows. This was not quite what my husband and I had in mind when our friends invited us to come see the "new house" they had just bought.

The barn had been weathered by storms, neglected, and vandalized. Over many years, it had stood derelict. But our friends had decided this was the perfect place to build their first home, where they would raise their soon-to-arrive baby.

1

"I'm not sure what to think," I responded nervously.

"Can't you see it?" they implored. They went on to describe a lovely family farmhouse with a large kitchen and living room and a nursery with a view. They explained how the house they envisioned in their hearts would be soon situated on this barren land.

Several years later, I sat in what is now a stunning farmhouse and ate in the large kitchen while taking in those breathtaking views. My friends' dream and dedication transformed that bleak hillside into a beautiful home.

Today I pose the same question to you: "What do you think?" You may not be standing on a barren hillside looking at a broken-down barn, but wherever you are in your life you find your own equivalent to that derelict building. Some of you may be experiencing brokenness in your relationships, a marriage that is struggling to survive, or a fragmented friendship that seems beyond repair. Others of you may be confronting addictions that have ravaged your loved ones or coming to terms with the loss of something or someone you held dear. Still others may be facing your once-robust business that is now failing. Daily we each awaken to our own equivalent of that broken-down barn, and daily we have to decide how to respond to the desolation we see.

Every day, you have to determine in your own heart, "What do I think?" What do you say in your spirit when you see the effects of the harsh storms of life? What is your conclusion when you look at our broken communities? How do you respond to the hardship and hostility on your streets? And how can you help transform the places you go to and help the people you meet?

I believe God is asking all of us the same question: *What do you think?* What are you saying and doing about the devastations you face? God has already envisioned the beautiful home He wants to build, the kingdom He will establish. God does not look at your desolation with doubt or at your ruins with timidity. He is your Creator God, the God of all sufficiency and grace.

He is the God who doesn't do slight improvements but who can completely turn things around.

> He is the God who doesn't do slight improvements but who can completely turn things around.

TURNAROUND POWER

In the beginning, God entered the darkness and displayed His turnaround nature. He spoke words that turned darkness into light and filled the emptiness with fruitfulness. His power brought order into the chaos. Our Creator God turned the dust of the earth into breathtaking birds of the air and into beasts of the field. He turned Adam's rib into his helpmate, Eve (Genesis 2:19–22). God revealed Himself as humanity's turnaround God—and ever since that moment, the enemy has sought to turn back what God has destined to turn around. From his first approach in the garden to Adam and Eve, the enemy came to manipulate and try to reverse God's turn. Sin entered and sought to stop every broken life being restored and every lost soul being found.

The enemy came to steal, kill, and destroy what God came to heal, find, and restore (John 10:10). God's turnaround power came in the form of His Son, who demonstrated once and for

3

all that there is nothing God cannot turn around. No death, no curse, no enemy can hold back God's turnaround power. The cross of Jesus Christ became the turning point for all humanity to receive their Savior. Christ took every bondage, sickness, and sin—and He paid the price to turn it around. He experienced death in order to attain life and freedom for us. God gave us the gift of a Savior who would reside within our lives. He took our lost eternity and gave us the choice to turn to Him and receive eternal life.

> ## No death, no curse, no enemy can hold back God's turnaround power.

We are now the custodians of that same turnaround power. As God's people, His Spirit rests within us. We are commissioned to work with Him to turn our world around, to speak into the darkness and bring forth His light, and to find those who are bound and bring them His gift of freedom. We have been given authority to turn around injustice with His justice and hopelessness with His hope. Yet often, we allow our doubts to question this power and let our fears contain this freedom.

We cannot allow our circumstances to compromise what Christ paid the highest price to attain. We must awaken our hearts, stir up our faith, and begin to look again at the places God has positioned us in. We need to see with new eyes the possibilities that our turnaround God can create in the places where no one else sees potential. We must seek to be the ones who bring answers where others only see problems. We need to shake off the complacency that can so quickly enter our hearts, causing us to settle for less than His Word promises.

> We cannot allow our circumstances to compromise what Christ paid the highest price to attain.

There is so much more for your life to embrace, so many breakthroughs for you to play your part in. We need a greater revelation of Whose we are, and in that understanding, we can grow a greater confidence of what He has called us to do.

TURNAROUND PERSPECTIVE

For most of my life, I have lived in the same city in England. Although surrounded by stunning countryside, the city where we are building our church and ministry is one of the most deprived and neediest parts of our country. Our city has become famous for all the wrong reasons: escalating crime rates, one of the highest-ranked cities in Europe for child poverty, and violent racial riots that have been watched in horror on global news networks. I would be lying if I said I have always loved living in my city. The truth is that on more than one occasion, I have asked God to relocate me somewhere less desolate and desperate.

I remember as a young girl going forward to many altar calls declaring, "Here I am, Lord; send me!" Yet my apparent willingness to be sent was tempered by a less apparent agenda of the places I would be willing to be sent to—and my hometown wasn't one of them. However, the greatest turnarounds always start from within our own hearts and lives. God tested me on many occasions in my willingness to stay where I was planted. Instead of looking for a way out, would I believe in a God who could turn things around?

> The greatest turnarounds always start
> from within our own hearts and lives.

When I married my husband, Steve, who happens to be American, he was living in the beautiful state of Washington. With its impressive mountain range and cascading waters, it presented stunning scenery year-round, from sweltering summers to snowy winters. I thought God had finally granted me my escape route. I would relocate not only cities but nations!

Yet God did not move me geographically; He moved me spiritually. Instead of giving me a great escape, He gave me a great turnaround partner in my husband, who felt God ask him to leave his idyllic backdrop and relocate with me to my needy city, which we now both call home. God began to show us the life He wanted us to build on this desolate hillside, the barrenness He wanted to fill with life, and the forgotten people toward whom He wanted to extend His love and kindness.

Our world needs to know the power of our turnaround God. But before it can experience this, we as God's people have to be able to visualize and articulate it. Going back to our friends on the bleak hillside . . . before I could get excited about their dream home, I had to be able to see what they could see. At first, I was focused on their risky investment, while they were enjoying the potential profit for their future. I was worried about the safety of their new baby, while they were dreaming of the space this would provide their expanding family. We were both looking at the same hillside but seeing and speaking out two very different conclusions.

So often it can be this way with our perspective and God's. While God is envisioning the "more than," we are focusing on the "less than." While He has seen the breakthrough, we are trying to decide if we will make it through.

TURNAROUND COMMITMENT

Most Christians would say amen to scriptures that speak of God's turnaround nature. We want to follow a God who can make the unlivable places livable again, who can bring prosperity to the land and restore it to its former glory (Isaiah 58:12). While we love to speak of God and His incredible power, and we may say amen and even teach the lessons, that does not necessarily mean we really believe it. It's only when we start to act on what we amen that we begin to discover how certain we are of God's turnaround ability.

> It's only when we start to act on what we amen that we begin to discover how certain we are of God's turnaround ability.

It was easy for me to say "go for it" to my friends' new building project because after I had said it, I could walk away from the actual responsibility of the project. The real test comes when you are the one who has to sign the contract for the land and dig up the earth, not knowing what you may find, and financially commit long-term to the investment. This is when the turnaround God is not just someone you have heard about but someone you are completely dependent upon. The depth of our understanding of our turnaround God often makes the difference between starting and completing. If we go into the desolate places to bring change only on the strength of a message we once heard, then when the desolation heightens, our commitment weakens.

> The depth of our understanding of our turnaround God often makes the difference between starting and completing.

As a pastor, I have seen many people commit to bring change because they were excited by the testimonies they heard. But sadly, on too many occasions, their commitment was cut short when their anticipated breakthrough didn't come quickly enough and the turnaround turned out to be harder than the "amen" in the service had led them to believe. Turnarounds don't happen overnight. God can give us one suddenly, but He also does slowly. He is committed to staying with the turn until it completely turns around, but He needs people who will commit to the process.

I remember our friends midproject, with the house going over budget and demanding overtime, and the baby coming sooner than planned. With no place to call home, the tension in their world mounted, and many people who had encouraged them to go for it now became critics, stating that they had taken on too much too soon. However, I remember how their clear vision silenced the panic during the hardest parts of their turn. They had the picture of their home in their hearts and looked at it regularly so that their temporary inconvenience wouldn't speak louder than their permanent gain.

This is one of the reasons I wanted to write this book. I have seen too many half-built homes, abandoned dreams, and unfinished projects. We embark into the desolate places with initial excitement. But if our understanding of God is limited and we do not find a deeper revelation of God's turnaround capacity, our excitement will wane. And when desolation shouts, we may be tempted to reduce our commitment, downsize our projects, and doubt the possibilities.

TURNAROUND ACTION

We need to understand our turnaround God because He speaks from a turnaround perspective. He may ask for actions that make no apparent sense to where we are currently living but make total sense for where we will be going. Have you ever felt God ask you to do something that seemed to make no sense? Maybe He asked you to sow financial seed when you were in a financial crisis. Perhaps He asked you to take on a new business venture when you were already stretched with your current business. Or God asked you as a parent to include more people into your already overstretched family. At times, God's counsel can seem insensitive or out of touch, so we misunderstand or even reject what we hear from God.

I remember the day my husband, Steve, and I went to what we thought was a regular doctor's appointment. We had gone to receive news of our recent test results. We entered the room laughing and chatting with the doctor to find ourselves only moments later sitting in complete silence at the news we had just received. My test had shown that I might not be able to conceive a child. Reeling from the casually delivered news, Steve and I left the office with our world now rocked and our faith about to be tested. During the next few months, we experienced a variety of emotions as we tried to seek God in this situation.

Then one day amid our tears we sensed God asking us to do something that seemed ridiculous. We felt God instruct us to throw baby showers for other people in our church who were pregnant; some of the people we barely even knew. I didn't feel like celebrating what I had been told I couldn't have, but I had to come to the realization that God was not being cruel to me. He was asking if I believed that He could turn anything around. If I did, then did that include my barrenness? Though I was unsure how God would bring about our miracle, I first had to start acting as if I believed God could provide a miracle. In my disappointment I had closed down every avenue for God's provision. I had closed my heart to the many ways in which this barrenness in my life could be removed. Therefore, I needed to start acting in accordance with my future and not my present.

This experience brought a new realization of why God would say in Isaiah 54:1, "Sing, barren woman, you who never bore a child; burst into song, shout for joy, you who were never in labor; because more are the children of the desolate woman than of her who has a husband." In this verse, God required an action that would begin the turning. By singing and shouting for joy, the barren woman was lining up with the promise and moving away from the problem. While you are singing, you can't be complaining, questioning, or moaning. God wanted the barren woman to hear a different sound. God wants all His people to sing in the struggle because they know barrenness is not the end but just the starting point of their turns.

> God wants all His people to sing in the struggle
> because they know barrenness is not the end,
> but just the starting point of their turn.

Jesus loved people. Yet if you always want His love to be expressed within your own personal levels of your sensitivity, you may feel let down. Jesus was criticized in the way He performed miracles, the days on which He would carry them out, and to whom He would extend them. The Bible is full of stories where God's answers seemed insensitive, where a prophet's behavior looked more crazy than sane, and where Jesus' ministry seemed careless and wasteful. One time, a prophet asked an influential ruler to wash in a dirty river, an instruction that was both disrespectful and insensitive to the ruler's position in the community (2 Kings 5). The prophet Elisha instructed a woman with nothing to go and find more emptiness that she would be required to fill (2 Kings 4). God told a starving widow who was about to use her last handful of flour and oil to feed her son a last meal to take those ingredients and feed a hungry prophet instead (1 Kings 17). Turnarounds by nature are radical; they bypass nice and sensible, they freak out the orderly, and they do not line up with agendas. But turnarounds reveal our miraculous Savior to our messed-up world.

Turnarounds reveal our miraculous Savior to our messed-up world.

Isaiah 54 continues to unfold God's counsel as He instructs the desolate to enlarge, stretch, expand, and advance (v. 2). God wants not merely a slight improvement for His people but a complete turnaround. We have to be careful that we don't downsize God's ability and become satisfied too easily.

I know how tempting it can be to take a small success as

the ceiling for what God wants to do. We are grateful for the two or three we have reached, but we can't allow that to become the capacity level at which we settle when God has the nations in His heart. We say size doesn't matter, but actually it does because we should be seeing people added to His church daily. We have to be careful not to downsize the Great Commission to one that is more manageable.

> We have to be careful not to downsize the Great Commission to one that is more manageable.

On too many occasions, I have allowed a sensible theology that said, "When the money comes in, then we will go out; when the right people join our ministry, then we will advance to reach more people." The enemy loves sensible planning, as it is no threat to his kingdom. If you downsize yourself, the enemy will become involved in your ministry, sending you more problems to manage and more people to help you keep things tidy. Yet there is nothing about God that downsizes, and He certainly isn't tidy! His strategies often do not seem sensible or His counsel logical.

God asked an elderly couple, who were ready for retirement, to have a baby. He instructed a stuttering shepherd to speak to Pharaoh and to deliver an entire nation. He told a boy on a hillside to leave the sheep and kill a giant. He chose a teenage girl to carry the Savior of the world. God doesn't downscale people; He supersizes them. He removes their comfort zones and throws them into the unknown, where His capacity overshadows their ability and they participate in the turnaround ministry of the God they serve.

Jesus came to turn the world upside down in the three years of His public ministry. He called a group of young men, mostly made up of teenagers, to come help Him turn around an entire world. He asked them to leave the tranquil lake for the sea of hurting humanity. Jesus' ministry was not safe; it was revolutionary. He came with miracles, not slight improvements—and often it was people's willingness to believe in His turnaround power that determined whether they went away healed and whole.

Jesus could have seemed insensitive when He said to cripples, "Get up and walk!" or to grieving relatives, "Open the grave!" His methods were questioned, but His miracles always brought answers. Turnarounds are not polite or politically correct; they are not people pleasing or protocol appeasing. Jesus wasn't trying to fit in; He came to turn things around. Throughout His ministry—in persecution, torture, misunderstanding, and betrayal—Jesus carried on undaunted, seeing a joy set before Him that would only be attained with a complete turnaround commitment. God sent us a turnaround Jesus and then gave us the turnaround facilitator, the Spirit of God.

> **Jesus wasn't trying to fit in; He came to turn things around.**

BECAUSE!

God's Spirit has a specific purpose that rests upon us. In Isaiah 61:1–3, we see that purpose explained:

> The Spirit of the Sovereign LORD is on me, *because* the LORD has anointed me to proclaim good news to the poor. He has sent me to bind up the brokenhearted, to proclaim freedom

for the captives and release from darkness for the prisoners, to proclaim the year of the LORD's favor and the day of vengeance of our God, to comfort all who mourn, and provide for those who grieve in Zion—to bestow on them a crown of beauty instead of ashes, the oil of joy instead of mourning, and a garment of praise instead of a spirit of despair. (emphasis added)

When we see the word "because" in this scripture, we must pay attention to it. The Spirit is not on us without purpose. God has given His Spirit to us as an enabler to turn around the most desolate circumstances, to bring those who are broken to wholeness and those imprisoned to freedom. The above is a list of the divine exchanges God wants to extend toward His people. He doesn't merely want to visit the captive; He wants to free the captive from all that has held him prisoner. He doesn't merely want to remove the ashes of grieving; He wants to replace those ashes with an extravagant crown of beauty. He wants those who are just getting by in life to know the God who is the giver of abundant life, by turning their hearts, minds, and spirits completely around. Therefore, we have to put the Spirit to work where we live, by finding those broken lives.

The Spirit is not on us without purpose.

We have to move among the imprisoned, the grieving, and the desolate in order for the Spirit to find the cause for which He was sent.

Every day on my way into work, I drive past a junkyard. I didn't even know it was there until recently, when one of our staff produced some incredible pieces of art for the church and informed me they came from material he had collected there. This staff member had gone to a place I'd only driven past, and he had taken what no one else wanted and made it into something beautiful. This is why the Spirit rests on us. God doesn't want His people to drive past the spiritual junkyards in our communities—the places where people have been left without hope, where they have been told they are worthless and nothing good can be made of their mess. He is looking for people who see what that staff member saw when he stopped at the junkyard. He saw potential and knew he could draw out something beautiful from what other people had deemed as awful.

I remember one time praying passionately for a person who was very sick to receive a miracle. Afterward, an older, and I presumed wiser, leader advised me to not pray with such strength and conviction, so as to avoid giving the sick person false hope. At the time I was confused. I thought that was why we prayed, to give people a hope that wouldn't disappoint and to lift our burdens to the One who carries what we cannot. I was praying to God, whom I knew to be greater than sickness, to the God who has given us power that can conquer the grave. I tried to understand this leader's perspective. I tried to appreciate this person's compassion and appeal for me to be more sensitive. Yet I couldn't reconcile how being sensitive meant downsizing what I believed a turnaround God could do.

THE TURNAROUND MANTLE

Salvation is a picture of how God's turnaround works. First, we have to see the turnaround from His perspective and experience it; then we become the facilitators of this turnaround to others. Those who have been turned around by God's love and power then become the turners. When we encountered Christ, our lives were completely turned around. Salvation turned our darkness into light, His forgiveness turned us from sinners to saints, and His intervention turned our focus from self to servant. He turned us around—but that was the first step. Now the Spirit awaits our participation. The desolate places await the arrival of God's turnaround people. Broken people are looking for turnaround believers to bring them crowns of beauty and to remove the ashes in their lives. Because of Christ, we now bear the turnaround mantle.

> **Because of Christ, we now bear the turnaround mantle.**

The scripture from Isaiah 61 we considered earlier ends in this way: "They will be called oaks of righteousness, a planting of the LORD for the display of his splendor. They will rebuild the ancient ruins and restore the places long devastated; they will renew the ruined cities that have been devastated for generations" (vv. 3–4).

As you read the following chapters, I want you to open your heart wide and begin to dream a bigger dream of what God can do and how He wants to use you to turn around the darkness. I want you to see that you are part of the great turnaround work God wants to do in the lives around you. Don't let anyone downsize your dream. Where do you need to remove limitations and receive a new vision of what God could do on your desolate hillside, in your barren land? Don't allow anyone or anything to convince you that God will do just enough when He wants to do more than enough.

> Open your heart wide and begin to dream a bigger dream of what God can do and how He wants to use you to turn around the darkness.

Too often we have settled where we could have soared; we have been content when we could have conquered. Don't let your spirit settle! I pray that this book makes you uncomfortable, challenges you, and motivates you to put your turnaround God to the test. I promise you, there is not one test He has failed yet. So keep reading as we commit afresh to keep turning!

TWO

TAKE YOUR TURN

ONE SUNDAY EVENING SERVICE IN OUR HOME CHURCH, I WAS completely undone as I sat with tears rolling down my face. I was overwhelmed as I listened to different people taking the microphone to testify to the amazing turns God had orchestrated in their lives. I listened as a nervous young man spoke of how only months earlier he had been homeless and hopeless, uncertain of where his next meal would come from, until the church entered with food and shelter and introduced him to his heavenly Father, who welcomed him home. He went on to share of how he now had a place to live, was applying for a job, and had finally found a place where he could belong. He was followed by a woman who spoke of how she had spent years battling addictions and escaping abusive relationships, but now her life had been completely

changed and she was drug free, in a safe and stable relationship, and, after years of separation from her children, about to
be reunited with them as they were being entrusted back into
her care. One after another, stories of God's incredible grace
and mercy moved everyone's hearts in the room that night and
revealed yet again the power of our Savior, who can take a life
from desolation to destiny, from broken to healed and whole.

On this same evening, as we were in awe of God's turnaround
power, I became aware that not only did God want to transform
the lives of the most desperate and hurting, but He had a turnaround for *every person* in the room. As I surveyed the auditorium,
I wondered how many of those sitting, applauding the stories of
others, were overlooking their own encounters with God. Too
often, we have reserved God's turnaround for those lives that seem
more desperate or hurting than our own. We can clearly see why
the heroin addict needs God to intervene and why the tormented
need their lives altered; yet when our own lives are less obviously
needy, we can begin to reason we are not desperate enough and so
don't qualify for God to reveal Himself in the same way.

> Too often, we have reserved God's
> turnaround for those lives that seem more
> desperate or hurting than our own.

TURN AVERSION

The more settled and satisfied we become in our lives, the more
we can develop a turn aversion. We gradually allow our satis-
faction to replace our seeking, and without the chaos crisis can

bring or the drive that despair places in our lives for God's intervention, we fail to see a need for God to transform anything around. Our lives can become like a rusting tap that gets stuck when it is only partially turned on; the flow of water running through it is far less than the tap's full capacity. God wants to be able to turn every life to the place where it finds its fullest flow and therefore discovers its greatest function. Our comfort becomes turn-averse; it acts like rust on the faucet of our lives, blocking our potential and opting to keep the disturbances to our comfort at a minimum. We downgrade the expectation of how we see God moving in our lives, and over time, our contentment becomes our containment.

> Over time, our contentment
> becomes our containment.

This happens as we misunderstand the reason and the way God works. He hasn't come to turn your world upside down; rather, He wants to turn your world right side up. We often think we know what our lives are supposed to look like, but God holds the blueprint. He has already seen each of our lives from the point of completion, and therefore we must allow Him to keep adjusting our building. The Bible likens our relationship with God to that of a potter and his clay. Jeremiah 18 says, "I went down to the potter's house, and I saw him working at the wheel. . . . Like clay in the hand of the potter, so are you in my hand" (vv. 3, 6).

We are called to be pliable clay in God's hands—and for that to work, we, like the clay, have to commit to the Potter's wheel. A potter uses his wheel to keep the clay constantly rotating. Turning is crucial to shaping an ordinary piece of clay into something magnificent that the potter has designed. The turning is not incidental to the process; it is crucial. Without the wheel, the clay becomes uneven and unshapeable.

An interesting thing about clay is if it is left off the wheel without anyone shaping it, the clay will revert to its previous form. The same is often true for our lives. Like that lump of clay, we have to stay on the Potter's wheel if we want to become all God has designed our lives to be. If we remove ourselves from the process, we can become rigid and settle back to our previous form. That form may be an old way of thinking, a limited mindset, or a restricted level of believing. Without the Master's hands continually moving in our lives, molding our course, we settle for a shape that is far less than what God had in mind.

I have seen a potter work at his wheel on several occasions, and I have even attempted, very unsuccessfully, to make something at the wheel myself. One thing that quickly became clear was if the wheel stopped turning, the clay was in trouble. That is why we must examine our understanding of how God works and not allow contentment to take us off the wheel. God is constantly turning the wheel to shape us, and we must embrace the process if we want to reach the potential the Potter has seen for our lives. Don't settle for being a teacup if God intended to make you into a vessel that could hold so much more!

The Bible tells the story of many dramatic turnarounds in people's lives, but it also catalogs turnarounds for people who were neither seeking nor expecting God to intervene. For a moment, I want to concentrate on those accounts, because those lives were not seemingly in need of a change. They weren't the cripple on the street corner crying out for help or the blind beggar asking God to change his world from one of darkness to light.

These turnaround stories were from ordinary lives. They were God's disturbing of the comfortable and turning of the settled. Maybe these stories are more akin to your life. Maybe you feel you have an ordinary life. The question is, are you overlooking what God wants to do in your life?

> Maybe you feel you have an ordinary life. The question is, are you overlooking what God wants to do in your life?

DECEIVER TURNED TO DELIVERER

Jacob was a young man who seemed to have it all—young, strong, adventurous, and adored by his mother, who showed clear favoritism toward him over his twin brother. Jacob lived a rich and full life. His mother helped him steal the birthright of the first-born from his brother, and he took the blessing that went with that honor. Jacob means "deceiver," and this is what he willingly became. Jacob was not seeking to give up his ways; he was content on many levels. But God wanted to turn things around in Jacob's world. He wanted to put Jacob's life in line with the blueprint He had designed for him, which was a complete change from where he was currently living.

God orchestrated Jacob back onto His Potter's wheel through a series of events that separated Jacob from his family so that he was alone with God. In Genesis 28:16, Jacob encountered the presence of God and the turning began. Jacob had allowed those around him to shape his life, and as so often happens when we leave the Potter's wheel, his life, although seemingly comfortable and content, was far short of what God had designed. Jacob began to go on a journey with God. He began working for Laban, a deceitful man—and as Jacob received unfair treatment from Laban, he realized how he had unjustly treated his brother, Esau.

Before this, Jacob had not recognized that he needed to change, but now the Potter was reworking the clay of his hardened heart. Jacob could have settled for a life far below the capacity this turnaround of events would prove he had. Jacob's attention became focused on the higher calling he was destined to live out. In Genesis 32, as Jacob is about to go back to meet his family after many years of separation, God makes one more turn as He asks Jacob a question: "The man asked him 'What is your name?' 'Jacob' he answered. Then the man said, 'Your name will no longer be Jacob, but Israel'" (v. 27–28). God wanted to transform the one named "deceiver" (Jacob) to see he was actually called to so much more.

Before God would allow Jacob to re-enter the land and reunite with the family he had left, He wanted to make the turn complete by letting Jacob know that he was not who others had said he was—he was not a deceiver; he was now Israel, the man who contended with God and triumphed. Like Jacob, we can live with a wrong label and become satisfied with an identity that doesn't match our Master's calling. It wasn't until Jacob got back onto God's wheel that he realized he had more options than the life he had settled for.

We can live under the wrong labels for years, allowing our environment to limit our destiny. Jacob was not seeking for God to change his life; he was not crying out for help. He was managing his own direction. But what if he had stayed a deceiver and never understood that he had a greater calling to fulfill? Jacob was asleep to his full potential, and we can also fall into the same trap. Where have you fallen dormant to the destiny within that your own wrestling with God will help you awaken?

TURNED FROM RETIREMENT HOME TO MATERNITY WARD

As they neared the grand old age of one hundred, Abraham and Sarah had given up any thoughts of having a baby. They were like any other couple in their retirement years, settling down for the slower pace of life. They had come to terms with their unfulfilled dreams and had decided their days of promises being answered were over. Their bodies were worn out and their expectations were lowered. The hopes of bearing their own promised child had died over time. What Abraham at one point was convinced God was going to do, he was now less concerned to see happen. Years earlier, Abraham's frustration with God's timing of their promised heir's arrival allowed him to take matters into his own hands, resulting in the birth of his son Ishmael through his servant Hagar.

This act of frustration became a source of much trouble and tension in his family for many years to follow. With his failed attempts to make things happen, Abraham conceded that Sarah would remain barren. The God who had said He would turn things around, Abraham decided, was not going to turn up. Now in his later years of life, he had buried his dreams and hidden his disappointments. Abraham and Sarah were faithful servants and lovers of God, but now at ages ninety-nine and ninety, they were busy planning their retirement. Yet God was not ready to send

Abraham and Sarah to the retirement home; His turnaround would send them heading to the maternity ward instead. God had not forgotten His promise and He was not bound by their circumstances. His promise, was going to be fulfilled when they were least expecting it and no longer even desiring it.

> God was not ready to send Abraham and Sarah to the retirement home; His turnaround would send them heading to the maternity ward instead.

Too often, like Abraham, we decide the ending before God does. We count ourselves out of God's turnarounds for reasons that make no difference to a God who has no limitations. Age was not a hindrance to God, nor was physical condition. God's selection is not based on any of the criteria we may create. God wanted Abraham to believe again and to be willing for Him to use his life at any stage to demonstrate His power. God called Abraham to get back in the game, a game he thought he was no longer needed to play a part in.

When God informed Abraham of His plans, Genesis 18:12 tells us that Sarah laughed out loud. Her mind was so closed to the miracle of carrying a child at her age that she laughed at how ridiculous it would be. Sarah wasn't looking to attend Lamaze classes at age ninety. But God wanted to use Sarah; He had not forgotten His promise to her. He had chosen her womb to carry this promised child, who would be named Isaac (meaning "laughter"). She was going to be a part of God's turnaround. Sarah would have to risk being ridiculous to embrace this next chapter of her life. She would have to sign back up where she had only seen herself signing out.

Maybe your life has gone into retirement planning. You may have hidden disappointments and settled into your golden years, but God wants you to remember that He can use anyone at any time; there is no age restriction. He just needs you to be willing to conceive again, and in that conception not only will your barrenness turn to fruitfulness, but your ending will be turned into God's new beginning.

WEAKEST TURNED TO WARRIOR

Another unlikely candidate for a turnaround was Gideon (Judges 6). Though his name means "mighty warrior," Gideon was anything but. He described himself as the weakest of the weak (v. 15). Happy to hide inside the cavernous wine presses, Gideon was more comfortable with grapes than people. His life was turn-averse, quiet, and contained. He didn't mind that he was off most people's radars; he liked being out of sight and out of most people's minds. This ordinary and unspectacular life would not seem to be the place for God to cause a turnaround. Gideon was not shouting, "Intervene!" He was pleading to be left alone. Yet God wanted to take Gideon from merely surviving to succeeding. He wanted Gideon to trade what was predictable for what was purposeful.

Spiritually, God knows what He has named you. He wrote before time what He predestined you to do. Yet so often we allow the circumstances of our lives to rename us. Failures, disappointments, hurts, and even successes begin to change our name, and we start to identify with the process rather than our purpose. Gideon had let his fears and environment rename him, so God came to remind him of what he was called to be.

Both times I was pregnant, we found out the gender of our child in advance. I have never been one for surprises and I am all about advance planning, so once we knew whether we were expecting a boy or girl, we decorated and purchased accordingly. This also gave us enough time to work on the important and sometimes daunting task of naming our soon-to-arrive baby. After reading many baby name books, Steve and I settled on the name Noah Brave for our son. Noah means "rest," and we loved the combination of bravery and rest. We prayed that our son would grow up to be a man who would be at rest with God and at rest with his strength.

However, when Noah was around age two, he decided his name was no longer Noah Brave and that he was now named George. He became obsessed with the name George, and we have no idea why. Every teddy was called George, and when we got a dog, we had to compromise and name him Jake George Gambill—he is probably the only dog with both a first and second name. It got to the point where Noah would only respond to "George" at home and at school. We had to sit down and explain to Noah that although George was a great name, it wasn't his name and that Noah Brave was what we had chosen to call him. It wasn't until we read Noah the story of Noah's ark that he decided it was actually a cool name, as what little boy wouldn't want to build a boat and have two of every kind of animal as his pets?

We can so often be like Noah Brave when it comes to what God has named us to be. As Noah's parents, we could have allowed him to carry on as George, but eventually there would come a point when he would have to face the fact that the identity he had chosen to live by and the identity on his birth certificate did not match up. There are times when we all need to examine whether we are living in keeping with what God has written on our spiritual birth certificates. Gideon had forgotten what his name means, and God had come to remind him in Judges 6 that he was called Gideon for a reason. His name means "mighty warrior," and that is what God was going to make him into.

> **There are times when we all need to examine whether we are living in keeping with what God has written on our spiritual birth certificates.**

Gideon was not looking to do anything heroic; he was happy hiding out and treading grapes. But God had a turnaround in mind. He was going to push past Gideon's turn aversion and challenge his perspective. God asked a scared, nervous man to "go in the strength you have" and save Israel (6:14). God threw Gideon back on His Potter's wheel. He called him to move from the winepress and go forward into a new adventure.

God knew where Gideon was hiding, and He knows exactly where you and I hide. He knows when we let the walls of the winepress shrink our destiny. He knows when we are fearful to move forward, so we stand still. God didn't wait for Gideon to climb out of the winepress and ask for His intervention, because He knew that day wouldn't come. So God brought to Gideon the opportunity to turn around, to go in the strength he already had and to discover who he already was—a "mighty warrior."

Maybe you need to let God change you from weakling to warrior; from fearful to faith-filled. Don't let your smallness make you turn-averse; rather, let it compel you to get on the Potter's wheel, knowing there is a larger vessel yet to emerge from your life.

Maybe you need to let God change you from
weakling to warrior; from fearful to faith-filled.

CONCUBINE TURNED TO QUEEN

Esther was just another pretty young girl to enter the king's harem. Like all the other girls, she was plucked from her familiar environment and placed in the most lavish of settings. With a twelve-month induction of beauty treatments, this orphan had her every need met. She had gone from a life of lack to a lifestyle of luxury, and she was quickly becoming accustomed to her new environment. Yet God had not called Esther to settle or to be pampered. He had called her for a much higher purpose.

Esther had many things obstructing her from being able or willing to make a turn. From her tender age, to her new status and the extravagance of her setting, Esther had no desire to disturb her life as one of the king's concubines. When her uncle Mordecai first informed Esther of the pending plight of the Jewish people, Esther's response let him know that she didn't see this as a problem she should try to resolve (Esther 4:10–11). Esther did not want to turn around and disrupt her new surroundings. But Mordecai was persistent and determined to awaken Esther to the reason God had placed her in the palace: "for such a time as this" (v. 14).

We are familiar with what came next. Esther's bravery and willingness to speak up for her people transformed her from concubine to queen. Yet this turnaround in Esther's life would not have happened if she had stayed in her comfort zone. Esther changed the fate of her people, but the first turn had to happen inside her own heart. Her first act of obedience meant exchanging comfort for confrontation and safety for the very real risk that her life could be taken. The first turn is often the most costly and therefore one we too often fail to make.

The first turn is often the most costly and therefore one we too often fail to make.

When I was younger, I remember going on a youth retreat, and when we arrived, everyone in the bus unloaded and ran into the hostel to find the best bed. In an attempt to find a place to sleep, my friend and I took the nearest option and settled down for the night. Satisfied with a warm room and a lumpy camp bed, we slept there for several nights. It wasn't until the last night at the camp that one of the girls from our room suddenly shouted out for us to come follow her. In an attempt to find a shortcut to the dining room, she had stumbled across a huge dormitory bedroom with real beds, clean sheets, and an in-suite bathroom that had been available all along for any of the youth to use if only they had been bothered enough to climb one more flight of stairs to discover it. I remember feeling such disappointment that we had settled for a lumpy camp bed with no bathroom, when if we had just walked a little farther, we could have moved from two-star accommodations to five. That is how it so often is with God's turnarounds.

Esther could have stayed in the harem where she had great accommodations; she had room service and spa treatments on demand. Yet God asked her to explore the next level with Him, to step out and go a little higher. Eventually, it was Esther's taking this turn that moved her from harem to honeymoon suite with the king. It opened up a new level of possibility not just for herself but also for all her people.

Don't let a lack of confidence deny you from what God has for you; don't let the lull of safety avert your next best step. Realize that even though you may feel no desperate need to turn, God's plan is so much bigger than you. Ultimately your willingness will be the key that frees many others to take their turns.

TURN IN ME

In an exquisitely made clock, each gear is overlapped and interconnected. All the cogs and wheels move in synchronization, making sure that everything is kept running in perfect time. When we fail to see the need for our cogs to turn, we deny all the cogs God has connected to our turnarounds their chances to move forward. God doesn't waste a single one. Jacob turned and a people were delivered. Gideon turned and a war was won. Esther turned and genocide was prevented. Imagine if any of them had averted their opportunities because they didn't see the need. We can't wait to turn based on our needs or fears or concerns; we must be willing to turn around and keep time with the One who holds all our times in His hands.

> We must be willing to turn around and keep time with the One who holds all our times in His hands.

So back to the night in my local church where the tears were flowing and the stories were being told, back to that room of applauding onlookers: I wonder who in that room was like

Jacob—a confident achiever, maybe the people's favorite, who hadn't realized that while he had achieved success in some arenas, he had no idea of the purpose and achievements that God had destined for him. He may have been sitting in the auditorium thinking he was "Jacob" while God was calling him to be His "Israel."

I wonder where the "Gideons" were, hiding inside that auditorium—the fearful ones, hesitant to leave the comfort zone they had come to feel safe inside. Which ones had become contained in a lifestyle far removed from where God was calling them to go? Who in that room had forgotten their true identity and had become more associated with weakness than the name their Father had given them of "mighty warrior"? And where sat the "Esthers"—the perhaps naive, the pampered, the satisfied, the ones who had settled in a place that took care of their needs, unaware they were being called to take care of the needs of so many more?

Not one person in the church that night was exempt from God's bigger plan. And not one of us can claim we are so put together or too messed up for God to turn our lives around and be what He has destined us to become. For some He has drastic turns; for others it is emotional; for others it may be a mind-set or a relational shift. But for every single person God has planned a turn that will cause their lives to go further and bless many more people.

> Not one of us can claim we are so put together or too messed up for God to turn our lives around.

We have to commit to throw our lives on the Potter's wheel and determine to enjoy the process. We embrace every turn, knowing that each time the wheel rotates, our vessels are taking shape and our capacity is being expanded. With every spin of the wheel, new possibilities open up, and we become more and more like the design the Master Potter always had in mind for our lives. Let's all take our turns on the wheel, for who but God knows what the next turn will bring?

THREE

STICKING POINTS

IN ENGLAND WE HAVE VERY NARROW ROADS, AS MY AMERICAN husband found out much to his horror. On his driving test, he discovered the road he was driving down the middle of was actually made for two cars! Needless to say, he veered into his lane quickly. In order to pass the driving test in England, you have to be able to do several things, including emergency stops, seamless gearshift transitions, parallel parking, and turning around your vehicle in as few maneuvers as possible. However, when it comes to this part of the test, the street you are on will determine the number of maneuvers you have to make to complete the turn.

We may believe in God to turn things around, but I wonder, how often have we secretly determined how many maneuvers within which we want to see a complete turnaround take place?

Are we like the driving examiner with our clipboard, marking God on the speed and smoothness of our transitions? The problem with this scenario is that we request turns with minimal maneuvers, but only God sees the road we are turning onto. Therefore only He can see just how many turns are required to stay on the path. We are not to test God but to trust God. Our job is to keep turning until God says drive on.

> **Our job is to keep turning until God says drive on.**

We must not get stuck midturn, for when we do we block the road and never move into the new direction that our lives are intended to take. There are many reasons we can get stuck, from weariness to frustration to stubbornness to disappointment. When the turn doesn't come as quickly as we had hoped, we need to know how to navigate our feelings so we don't jeopardize our futures. Let's examine a few places where we can get stuck.

FROZEN IN FEAR

Elijah was a prophet of God of whom many stories are told in the Old Testament. He was a man who fought against the false gods and idol worship of his day. He was a passionate prophet who often delivered God's Word with signs and wonders. On one such occasion Elijah had just called down fire, he had taunted the false god Baal, and then to finish off, he had outrun a chariot (1 Kings 18). So the last place we would expect to see Elijah after this impressive set of events was lying under a tree, asking for his life to be taken from him. Yet Elijah was so depressed and worn out that he asked God to take his life; in his weariness he let his feelings navigate him to this place of resignation (1 Kings 19:3–5). He had allowed the fear of his pursuing enemy to overwhelm his faith.

Elijah did not want any more trouble. Yet God never promised that our turnarounds would be trouble free. We have to understand that all God's turnarounds will at some point create some trouble. In fact, when we start working with God to turn things around, it's like sending out an invitation for trouble to show up. We just don't know when trouble will respond to the invitation. It's just like digging in a garden: you may dig up several mounds of soil and disturb nothing, but eventually there will be one shovelful that will dislodge an annoyed insect or awaken a sleeping worm. Elijah's obedience became some people's disturbance. King Ahab, to whom God sent Elijah, even called Elijah the "troubler of Israel" (1 Kings 18:17). We have to be willing to make the right kind of trouble for God and be prepared for when that trouble starts to respond.

All God's turnarounds will at some point create some trouble.

If we inherit trouble out of obedience to God, we can rest assured He is our defender. But at the news that trouble was pursuing him, Elijah was frozen by fear that left him sitting under a tree. Fear of what could happen often prevents us from discovering what can happen. Elijah was not finished doing what God had asked him to do; there were more maneuvers to be made to turn around the nation. Yet because of the threat of his enemy, Elijah was frozen in fear.

> ## Fear of what could happen often prevents us from discovering what can happen.

Some people miss their turns because of fear: the fear of the unknown, the fear of failure—all these can freeze our lives and prevent our turns. We have to examine if we are allowing fear to freeze us. God sent an angel to Elijah to get his life moving again. God wanted Elijah to turn around and get back on track with the maneuver he was mandated by heaven to make: "The LORD said to him, 'Go back the way you came, and go to the Desert of Damascus. When you get there, anoint Hazael king over Aram. Also, anoint Jehu son of Nimshi king over Israel, and anoint Elisha son of Shaphat from Abel Meholah to succeed you as prophet'" (1 Kings 19:15–16).

God had a destiny in mind for Elijah that would ensure his legacy was carried on in strength. Elijah had successors to anoint and servants to train; God would not allow Elijah's turn to terminate under a tree. God had an ending for Elijah that included chariots of fire and double anointing! We, too, must not allow fear to compromise how we finish, for God will always finish the turns He starts. Like Elijah, we may experience periods of panic and temporary confusion, but we can't stop in the moment or we will allow fear to freeze us.

> ## We, too, must not allow fear to compromise how we finish, for God will always finish the turns He starts.

Maybe you are stuck in your turn, are frozen in fear, and don't even realize it. Maybe the lack of progress in your life is not because God is holding you back but because fear has created a prison in which your potential remains locked. God told Elijah to get up and get back out on the road God had originally placed him on. The problem with getting stuck midturn is that it doesn't just hold you up; it holds back everyone else from taking their turns. Until Elijah completed his turn, no succession could begin; no anointing and commissioning could take place. Elijah's moment of selfishness under the tree could have jeopardized the turns of many more people.

When I was younger, I had a lead role in a school production, and I had the unenviable task of remembering pages of dialogue for my first performance. I had rehearsed in such a way that other people's lines always triggered mine. If they failed to speak their lines, I would not be able to speak mine. I remember on opening night things were going really well until one of the cast got stage fright and stopped midsentence. Instead of trying to recover, the student just crumbled with fear. The problem only got worse because her line led into mine; but without her saying her lines, I was unsure of how to say mine. For those few agonizing moments, which felt like hours, no one moved, no one spoke, and everything was frozen in time. The silence was eventually broken as a prompter spoke the lines I had been searching for.

One person's fear almost stopped the whole performance. Spiritually we must also deal with our stage fright, so we don't hold up those whose turns are connected to ours. The Holy Spirit acts like that stage prompter; when fear comes to stop you, the Spirit speaks the lines you are searching for. The angel came to Elijah to prompt him back into his part and get his life unstuck again (1 Kings 19:7).

Fear is real, but we must learn to isolate its power. If fear has frozen you, allow God's presence to thaw you, and listen for the

Spirit's prompting that reminds you there is more work to do before you are allowed to catch your chariot home.

STICKY STUBBORNNESS

If you had to record your life's journey for all time in four chapters in the Bible, what would you write? I am sure we would all choose to recall the moments when we triumphed, when we saw breakthroughs. We would probably give full detail of our victories while glossing over our failures. Not Jonah; he wrote an account of his life that included not his greatest successes but his greatest moments of stubbornness, where his life got so stuck he ended up inside the belly of a whale for three days.

Jonah's story is a classic tale of how stubbornness can stop our turnarounds with God. When God called Jonah to facilitate a transformation in the land of Nineveh, God uncovered in Jonah a sin he had kept concealed. Jonah refused to make this turn because, as we find out in chapter 4, Jonah had a prejudice against the Ninevites, feeling that their compromise and sin made them unworthy of God's grace. There are times we can become stuck because we, like Jonah, have areas of our hearts we have shut down to God's turnarounds. We have secret prejudices, places we do not wish to go to, people we don't want to reach. God asked Jonah to take a turn to Nineveh because He knew Nineveh was going to make the biggest turn inside Jonah's own life.

> God asked Jonah to take a turn to Nineveh because He knew Nineveh was going to make the biggest turn inside Jonah's own life.

Maybe like Jonah, the thought of going to some places and people groups has you heading in the opposite direction. If Nineveh is in your future, you can run but you can't hide from it, as Jonah found out. God will not let you stay stuck in your stubbornness even if He has to send a storm to get you unstuck. Stubbornness can cause us to be stuck for a long time, and often the only way you can get unstuck is to surrender.

As a child my dad would often wrestle with my three sisters and me. He would eventually pin us in a headlock. (I know it sounds rather cruel, but we found it fun at the time!) Once in the headlock the only way out was if we shouted, "I surrender!" My sisters would spend no more than a few seconds in this uncomfortable position, but I was another case entirely. I would stay in that place for a long time trying to free myself, unwilling to give in and admit defeat. I would try anything but say, "I surrender." My stubbornness only prolonged my agony and kept me stuck. It's the same for our spiritual journeys. Our stubbornness doesn't avoid the turn; it just prolongs the storm God sends to redirect our lives back on track.

Where are you too stubborn to be sent? Our church has taken God's turnaround message to places that at times have stretched the most willing and committed church volunteers. We have gone to the pimps and prostitutes, to the abused and the abusers, to the victims and the perpetrators. We have to be careful not to have a belief that sees great value in turning to the ones who have been wronged but not turning to reach the ones who are causing the wrong. If we are truly going to see a turnaround in our world, we have to turn up in everybody's world.

If stubbornness has gotten you stuck, then like Jonah, expect God to send a storm; and like Jonah, know that God will ask you to surrender by going overboard where He will add another point to your turn that involves a whale. Jonah had to get in that whale not because he couldn't swim but because God had more turning for him to do. Scripture says that "the LORD provided" the whale (Jonah 1:17). Even the choice of Jonah's language shows that in hindsight Jonah had a new appreciation for the fish that swallowed him, as it was in the whale where he had his own headlock moment with God until he finally said, "I surrender."

Jonah prayed from the belly of the whale a prayer that turned his heart and surrendered his stubbornness:

> *In my distress I called to the LORD,*
> *and he answered me.*
> *From deep in the realm of the dead I called for help,*
> *and you listened to my cry.*
> *You hurled me into the depths,*
> *into the very heart of the seas,*
> *and the currents swirled about me;*
> *all your waves and breakers*
> *swept over me.*
> *I said, "I have been banished*
> *from your sight;*
> *yet I will look again*
> *toward your holy temple."(Jonah 2:2–4)*

It took three days and three nights until Jonah said, "I surrender!" There are some turns where we have to tell God, "I surrender. I don't want to go, but I need to go."

We also decide how long we get stuck. Jonah spent three days inside the stinky belly that stubbornness placed him in, but his release was found in his turning to the people of Nineveh. With one action Jonah was unstuck, as the whale vomited him onto the shore of the very place he had been avoiding. Jonah's refusal to go to Nineveh didn't change God's commitment to send him. His stubbornness didn't change the direction; it just delayed his arrival.

Jonah was now on his way to offer an entire nation an opportunity to turn. As he walked into Nineveh, he had the aroma of whale vomit all over him. The whale vomit was not an incidental part of this story—Jonah could have left out that humiliating detail, but whale vomit was not something you saw every day. It was not in a whale's nature to vomit, much like it was not in the nature of a meat-eating raven to carry meat to feed a prophet, nor was it in a donkey's nature to talk, or a lion's nature to let a young man sleep on him instead of eating him. But for the turnaround God, everything is potential turnaround material.

This whale vomited out Jonah at God's request. Jonah landed in Nineveh fragrant from his whaling experience. The aroma from the whale would have clung to his clothes for quite some time, reminding Jonah of the lengths God had gone to turn him around. It is worth noting that the fragrance of whale vomit changes over time, and it is a valuable ingredient in exclusive perfumes around the world. The whale vomit, though it may have seemed worthless, was actually of high value. So our turnaround encounters with God may at times feel pointless, yet over time we will come to realize they are priceless.

Jonah entered the whale when stuck in his stubbornness and exited the whale with the aroma that only a surrendered life can eventually bring. Once Jonah took his turn, it wasn't long until the nation of Nineveh followed and turned to God.

DISAPPOINTMENT DIVERSIONS

Disappointments happen to us all, but we don't all respond to them the same way. Learning to deal with disappointment is crucial if we are going to keep making the turns God has for our lives. We can't ignore or avoid disappointments; the fact is, people can let us down, family and friends can fail us, and at times we can mistake disappointments for God letting us down.

If we can learn from anyone about how to avoid disappointment diversions, we can learn from Job. Job was a faithful servant of God, a successful businessman known for his generosity and integrity. God allowed the enemy to test Job, such was His confidence in Job's faithfulness.

Job wasn't superhuman; he didn't have any inside information that kept him on track when everything around him was falling apart. But he had a tenacious faith that clung to God in every trial and tribulation. When Job's life took a turn that no one expected, his friends offered Job diversions from the path he was on. His friends, whom Job aptly called "miserable comforters" (Job 16:2), suggested Job's lifestyle must have caused God to punish him. They tried to figure out why Job had so offended God that He would subject him to such punishment. Even Job's wife, reeling from pain and turmoil, told Job to "curse God and die" (2:9).

Job couldn't find one person to encourage him in his plight, as he expressed in Job 16: "I have heard many things like these; you are miserable comforters, all of you! Will your long-winded speeches never end? What ails you that you keep on arguing? I also could speak like you, if you were in my place; I could make fine speeches against you and shake my head at you. But my mouth would encourage you; comfort from my lips would bring you relief" (vv. 2–5).

Job found disappointment a lonely place. His success had seen many friends attach to his life, but his disappointment saw just as many leave. Often we can let disappointment isolate us from others; we can feel rejected, forsaken, and overlooked. During those moments the enemy can divert our lives from what will eventually be one of the greatest turnarounds of all time. Job did not know that the end of his story would see God trade every pain into prosperity, every loss into gain. But he did know that God was still on track even if his life plan wasn't. Job 2:9–10 says, "His wife said to him, 'Are you still maintaining your integrity? Curse God and die!' He replied, 'You are talking like a foolish woman. Shall we accept good from God, and not trouble?'"

Job's wife pointed out that Job was still holding on to his integrity. In the face of disappointment, we often let go of our integrity, the values we said we would never compromise, the vows we promised to keep. These become tested when others fail to keep their word or uphold the commitments they swore to fulfill. We can allow others' lack of faithfulness to temper our own, and we question why we should give our best if others are not reciprocating. We start to go back on our commitments, undo our confessions, and doubt our beliefs. Because we feel let down, we allow that to be our permission to let others down. But if we want to avoid the diversion of disappointment, we must hold on to the same values and beliefs and trust God to take us from trouble to triumph.

There have been many occasions on my journey when disappointment has almost cost me a very damaging diversion, when I have doubted God because something didn't happen when I thought it should. There have been times when what I prayed and fasted for never happened. I remember praying for a job I had set my heart on. I asked my friends to pray with me. I had decided this was the job for me. Yet I didn't get the job; I wasn't even called for a second interview. I was so disappointed. I questioned the point of fasting and praying when I hadn't gotten the results I had requested. Little did I know that the job loss was a blessing from God, as the job I hadn't even dared to ask or pray for was offered to me a few weeks later. God could see the turn that was further up my path, but all I could see was the disappointment that almost diverted me from what was ahead. Similarly, Job could have cursed God; he could have blamed others. Instead, he knew the God he served could take anything and turn it around, so he held on to his integrity and kept moving forward. We finally read in Job 42:12: "The Lord blessed the latter part of Job's life more than the former part."

Don't let disappointment stop you short of your turn. Don't get stuck in your sorrow or hung up on your hurt. Hold on, push forward, and trust the turnaround God, who can make your latter days even better than your first.

> Hold on, push forward, and trust the turnaround God, who can make your latter days even better than your first.

FACING FAILURE

Nobody sets out to fail. We all desire to do our best in life and see some level of success. We set out on our journeys praying and believing for God to help us achieve our goals and reach the targets we have set for ourselves. So when a hoped-for outcome doesn't happen, when we don't achieve the grade or get the job, then we face one of the biggest obstacles in our ability to turn: we face failure. We have to deal with the reality that we may have to retake that exam or apply for another job. We have to find the motivation to try again, believing that this time we may succeed. Failures, however big or small, are something we all have to learn to navigate; otherwise, the place where we fail will become the place where we stop.

> Failures, however big or small, are something we all have to learn to navigate; otherwise, the place where we fail will become the place where we stop.

As a parent I have realized the importance of teaching our children how to celebrate success and not fear failure. When our daughter was younger, she used to hate joining in with any competitive activities at school. On the family sports day, she was reluctant to enter any of the races; when we asked her why she didn't want to take part, she told us it was because she didn't want to fail. She knew the other girls in her class were faster runners, so rather than try and fail she preferred to not even get on the starting line. I explained to her that to try and fail was better than failing to try. Just as she could grow from her achievements, she could also improve through her failures. When we talk about only our success, we feed a very real fear of failing that can create a braking effect on our turnarounds. Failure can bring to an abrupt halt the journey on which God has called you to be.

One of the heroes of the faith is Moses, the Hebrew boy who

grew up to deliver God's people. Moses confronted Pharaoh, parted the Red Sea, and led the Israelites to the promised land at God's command. Moses succeeded in many ways, but he also faced failure. When Moses was still living in Pharaoh's household, he saw an Egyptian mistreating one of the Hebrew slaves, and in a fit of outrage Moses took the Egyptian's life. This failure caused Moses to run away from God's calling. He let his mistake grind him to a halt. He fled to the desert, where he parked his destiny and put a handbrake on his dreams, letting his failure define him. So God broke into Moses' world and reminded him that his failure was not his final destination. He was called to turn around a nation. He couldn't stop midway; he had to get back up, go back to the place where he had failed, and start again.

When Adam and Eve failed in the garden of Eden by eating from the tree of life, their first response was to hide from God. They felt ashamed and unworthy to be seen or used by God, yet God came to where they were hiding and reminded them of their turnaround mandate. He would not let their failing cut short their turning. Jesus did the same for His disciple Peter.

Jesus had warned Peter of his pending failure of denying Christ three times, but Peter could not accept this would take place. He confessed over and over again his commitment to Jesus. Yet a few days later Peter denied over and over again that he had ever met this same man, Jesus. Peter, reeling from his failure to stand his ground and confess his faith, felt such shame at his denial that he let his failure halt his progress. He went back to his old life as a fisherman. He sat down in his boat mindful of his mistake and letting go of his ministry. Peter had failed, but Jesus was not finished with Peter. Jesus knew the failure was coming, yet He still planned to use Peter as the turnaround apostle of the early church. Jesus re-entered Peter's world to put him back in the place where his failure had caused him to leave.

In the same way, we must learn from our failures and keep turning back to God. When we fail in any area, whether it is a job or a relationship, we have to find the strength to try again. When I first took my driving test, I remember getting to the end of the ordeal only for the examiner to tell me I had failed. That verdict not only destroyed my confidence but also restricted my lifestyle, as I was now unable to get a license to drive. I didn't want to let my failure keep me from enjoying the freedom that passing my test could bring. So as soon as I found out I had failed, I applied to retake the test. Because of my persistence, the second time I passed, and I gained a license and the freedom I would never have gained if I had allowed my initial failure to be the final decision. If we stop our turnarounds every time we fail, our progress will be delayed and our mission will never be accomplished. Failure happens, but it doesn't have to be the final statement about your future.

> Failure happens, but it doesn't have to be the final statement about your future.

OBSTACLES OF OFFENSE

"Off with his head!" was the cry of Herodias, King Herod's wife, when her young daughter was presented with an opportunity that could have turned a nation around. Herodias's daughter had danced for the king and all his officials, and as a reward for her pleasing them she was offered the gift of having any request granted, up to half the kingdom. That was quite an offer for a young girl with her whole future ahead of her. This was an opportunity for Herodias's daughter to take her turn and do something extraordinary with her life. She could have turned her kingdom from one of oppression to freedom; she could have changed laws, acquired resources, fought injustices, and created a better future for her generation. Yet in her moment, when it was her time, she instead sought the counsel of her offended mother. Mark 6:24 says, "She went out and said to her mother, 'What shall I ask for?' 'The head of John the Baptist,' she answered."

Herodias had nursed a grudge against John the Baptist for years, ever since he had questioned her unlawful marriage to Herod. Her husband put John the Baptist in prison to appease his wife's incessant nagging for John to be punished. But she would not let it go, and as time went on, the offense grew. With every year, her hatred of John deepened and her resolve for revenge strengthened. Mark 6:21 tells us, "Finally the opportune time came" for Herodias's offense to have its way, as the daughter's moment of favor could be used to fulfill the mother's vendetta.

Just as God wants you to take your turn, the enemy is just as committed to make you miss it—or even better yet, misuse it. The enemy is often extremely active during pivotal turning-point decisions. Herodias's daughter, unaware of the significance of the moment, allowed her mother's offense to obstruct her path. Her failure to take her own turn afforded her mother an opportunity to take it for her—with devastating consequences. Herodias's daughter allowed the past offenses of her mother to steal the opportunities of her future. The enemy can slow down a turnaround with the power of offenses.

The enemy can slow down a turnaround with the power of offenses.

Offenses have the power to create obstructions that can be so large they can prevent turns being made for generations. Proverbs says, "A brother wronged is more unyielding than a fortified city" (18:19). Such is the shutdown power of an offense. We must guard our hearts from the many offenses and agendas that can be placed in our paths. We can't allow our hurts to hijack our lives. The reality is we are all going to be hurt, and at some point we all will cause an offense because there is no such thing as a perfect person. But we don't have to become obstructed by our offenses. We don't have to get stuck in the tightening grip of an insult that is holding us back from taking a turn. We must live with enough passion to push past our desire to park until we feel we have been avenged.

Imagine years later, as this young woman looked back over her life and the next generation asked her what difference she made, what turnaround she navigated—all she would have to show for herself was the head of a man who once offended her mother. We must awaken our hearts and be alert to our turns. Don't settle for a head when you could have up to half the kingdom.

OIL CANS

Whether it is fear, disappointment, offense, or stubbornness, we must not get stuck in our turns. We must keep maneuvering as God keeps moving. Have you ever gotten stuck in a revolving door? This happened to one of my children at a hotel we were staying in. The door was very heavy and rather old, and I think it had had enough of people swinging it around on its creaking hinges. My child went in the door but halfway around got stuck in the turn.

Perhaps as you have read this chapter, you have realized you are stuck in your turn, trapped between where you began and where you need to go. The doors have closed around you and your life feels as though it cannot move any more on those tired, creaking hinges. Yet your journey doesn't have to end that way. The solution to every place where we have become stuck is to bring out what the manager of the hotel called his "special bottle." He produced for this panicking parent's relief a bottle of oil that was reserved for such occasions. As he applied the oil, the hinges eased, the door loosened, and the turn began again until my child was released at the other side to my relief and delight.

Just a little oil loosened a small hinge that created a huge release. It is often easier to get unstuck than we realize. We just have to apply the oil to the hinges of our lives. If fear has frozen you, apply the loosening power of His perfect love; if stubbornness has shut you down, embrace the oil of sweet surrender. If you are stuck in disappointment, apply the oil of gratitude; if you're stuck in offense, apply the oil of forgiveness. We need to commit to keeping our lives well oiled. When we feel that our progress is creaking and our commitment is sticking, we need to know how to draw from God, how to stay in a place where we know His mercies to be new every morning, His grace to flow freely to us, and His love to cover every part of our lives. Don't dry up, withdraw, or stay stuck, like my child who felt alone and confused between those doors. In the moments when we get stuck, we can also become isolated and confused. We can forget this is not our end point; this is just one part of the turn.

As my child began to panic, I called to him and we locked eyes. In that moment, though he was stuck, he knew I was not leaving his side until he was free. The same is true in our relationship with God. Take the time to look up from where you have become stuck and catch His eye that is ever on you. God will help you get free. Just as I was waiting eagerly for my child at the other side of those doors, so God and many others are waiting for you when you continue your turnaround. For your sake, and for theirs, oil your life today and keep turning.

FOUR

TURN THE
OTHER CHEEK

ONE OF MY MOST EMBARRASSING AND HUMOROUS MOMENTS took place one summer day in England. It started as my mom and I were heading out for the day in her car. We were already running late, so when we came to the end of our road, we were frustrated to find a huge traffic jam. We lived in a small country village. To encounter any traffic was unusual, so it concerned us that this line of vehicles was not going to be moving any time soon. Several frustrated drivers had gotten out of their cars to see what the holdup was and indicated it would be a long wait. So with no way to exit the one-way lane of traffic, we noticed a car a few places down had pulled out of the line and was going down a small side alley. It was at that moment that my mum and I made what would later prove the worst decision possible.

In a reaction to our frustration at the traffic, hoping the driver knew a shortcut that we didn't, we pulled out of the lane of traffic and followed this complete stranger's car. At first, we were temporarily relieved by the fact that we were finally moving somewhere. But that relief was to be short lived, as we soon realized, horrified, that we had just driven up the side of a canal embankment and were now driving illegally down a footpath made for people and their dogs, not cars.

As we drove down this ever-narrowing footpath, we were clearly following someone who didn't live in the countryside and had made a very poor error of judgment. However, we had no choice but to continue on. Soon we began to pass casual Saturday afternoon walkers who had hoped for a peaceful stroll with their young families. They now stood close to the edge of the water, in fear for their safety as our car came toward them, leaving no room to pass. Irate joggers started shouting at our car and one annoyed elderly gentleman hit our car with his walking stick, as he had nearly been knocked into the canal. As my sweet and very embarrassed mum drove along apologizing to all the people, I chose to cowardly crawl on the car floor and place a coat over my head.

Then the terrible realization dawned that there was no way through this footpath. We arrived suddenly at a dead end! There was only one option—yes, you guessed it: we had to turn our vehicle around and drive all the way back up the canal path past the same people we had just endangered and annoyed. That long drive back seemed to take forever as abuse was hurled at our vehicle, including our car being hit again with the same walking stick. Eventually we made it back off the path at the exact point we had entered it. This damaging detour of over thirty minutes resulted only in us going right back and joining in at the end of the now-increased traffic jam we had impatiently just left.

I now live with my family right next to this canal embankment. We often walk our dog along the same footpath, and every time we walk I recall this story. I am astounded as to how we fit a car along that path without seriously injuring anybody or ending up in the water ourselves. This ridiculous story demonstrates what it often looks like to live a life with unforgiveness. When we are hurt or offended, we have a choice to make. We can stay with God's plan to let forgiveness turn our hearts and wounds around, or we can let the enemy use our hurts to hijack our lives. At first, allowing your hurts to choose your direction may seem inviting. Expressing anger or bitterness appears easier, just like our detour did initially; but the path that unforgiveness leads you down will cause a lot of damage to your life and the lives of others. Unforgiveness ultimately takes you to a dead end where you will stay until you allow the transformative power of forgiveness to turn your life in the right direction.

> When we are hurt or offended, we have a choice to make. We can stay with God's plan to let forgiveness turn our hearts and wounds around, or we can let the enemy use our hurts to hijack our lives.

Forgiveness is one of the hardest and yet most powerful attributes of our turnaround God. Yet if we are going to embrace His full power we cannot leave this subject uncovered. Even though we may not feel like it, forgiveness is a crucial part of our lives. When Christ went to the cross, He did not go because He felt like it. He went because this display of forgiveness was the turn that would ensure our salvation. Without the turnaround act of forgiveness, there would be no hope, no eternity, and no freedom. Though the cost of the cross was indescribable, the rewards were indefinable. The price tag of forgiveness may seem at times too much to ask, but the truth is, unforgiveness always costs more than anyone should be willing to pay.

Salvation is based on the turning power of God's forgiveness and is activated by the turning action of our repentance. *Repentance* may be deemed by some as an old-fashioned word, but it's a word we need to know and understand. Repentance is a turning from sin. Our life with God begins with the turning action of repentance. But it doesn't stop there. It is our willingness to keep turning from sin that ensures our ability to keep moving in the right direction. His forgiveness is in constant supply, yet our unwillingness to repent can make its flow inconsistent. Before God ever asks His people to turn around anything externally, He requires our commitment to keep turning our lives internally.

SORRY AND SURRENDER

Our son once went through a phase at school where he was always getting in trouble for the same crime; it seemed his soccer tackles at recess were a little too zealous. After he had made countless apologies to both teachers and injured teammates I began to realize that as his parents we were not making much progress with this behavior. Yes, our son was sorry, but he was not willing to surrender his aggressive behavior. My son fell into the trap that too many of God's kids are still stuck in: he believed saying sorry would fix the problem. But his sorry was like attaching a Band-Aid to a seeping wound. He didn't need a temporary improvement; he needed a permanent change. Saying sorry, like putting on a Band-Aid, can appear to make things better. It covers over the wound, but nothing has been changed underneath. Repentance, however, is the commitment to turn from the behavior that keeps irritating the wound so the healing can be permanent. God calls not for an apology but for action. Repentance does not speak; it moves. It stops the behavior; it changes the company; it turns away from the sin and starts walking in a completely new direction.

After several long conversations with us, our young son moved from sorry to surrender. He stopped apologizing and started turning. He had to stop playing at recess with the boys who encouraged his aggressive tackles, he had to learn at age five how to control his temper, and he started to follow through on his commitment to change. To his delight and our relief he soon found no need to keep apologizing or enduring time-outs. He became more confident and much happier; he had better friends, better recess, and even better soccer scores. His surrender took him to a place his good intentions never could.

LESSONS FROM A KING

King David, known as a man after God's own heart (Acts 13:22), had an exemplary record of serving God and His people. He was loved and supported by many. So when David committed adultery with Bathsheba, he was well aware that this mistake could tarnish his reputation and threaten his kingdom. This one action of sin was about to take him on a devastating detour that an act of repentance could at any time turn around. Yet instead of surrendering his pride and seeking forgiveness, David tried to maintain his position and took matters into his own hands. David took a detour by trying to make his own way out of the situation his sin had created. To David, rerouting was more appealing than repenting, so he let his pride talk him out of his turnaround.

David's initial mistake led to many more mistakes as his detour created collateral damage. Bathsheba discovered she was pregnant with David's child, and on hearing this news, David tried to apply more Band-Aids to the increasingly infected wound. He tried to cover his sin by bringing Bathsheba's husband, Uriah, home from war to be with his wife. Yet Uriah, a righteous man, refused to turn away from his duties on the battlefield for a night with his wife. So David, still refusing to repent, continued on his destructive detour and arranged Uriah's murder. Finally, after David's many failed attempts to fix things, he cried out to God when the son he had conceived with Bathsheba died—yet another casualty from the path he had chosen. David could have altered his course at any time; he could have turned around and avoided ending up in what was now a literal dead end.

We must examine our own lives and ask, how long does it take for us to repent and turn from the detours our sins can cause? When have we tried to fix with our sorry what only our repentance can redeem? We all come off track, but we don't have to stay there. We have the power at any time to stop and change direction. We have to take account of the damage our hesitancy to turn can cause and determine to not waste time in places where God never intended to send us. When David eventually came to his senses and turned to God, he found He was not slow to respond. God took David from his place of mourning and gave him a reason for rejoicing by opening Bathsheba's womb again to conceive their son Solomon. David turned to God, and God turned his life around.

What God did for David He will do for you and me. There is no place His forgiveness will not flow, no dead end from which He cannot deliver you. We cannot allow fear or shame to hold us back from His forgiveness; we must not allow our mistakes to become our address. God wants you to embrace the forgiveness that will keep moving you forward.

> God wants you to embrace the forgiveness that will keep moving you forward.

BETTER TOGETHER

Without forgiveness, we lose our momentum. When we allow hurts to hinder our progress or offenses to take us off course, we lose the impetus we require to keep turning things around in our lives and the lives around us. We have to be aware that the more people we try to help, the more we can potentially be hurt. And the more we give, the more we may be taken advantage of. Therefore, our defense against allowing these things to detour us is our ability to forgive. We have to find the strength to look past what potentially could hold us back.

Jesus came to turn people's lives around, and an important part of turning around is finding forgiveness. Jesus healed the sick, restored the broken, and gave sight to the blind, yet still He was falsely accused. The same people He helped had Him cruci-fied, and even those closest to Him betrayed and denied Him. Yet Jesus never gave up on the people who gave up on Him. He never retaliated or sought revenge. He didn't quit through disap-pointment or take offense at the denials. Jesus was able to move forward, reach people, and continue to bless because when hurts came knocking at His life, He sent forgiveness to answer the door. Jesus knew that the fuel of forgiveness was something all those who follow Him would need. He told His disciples in John 15:21 that those who tried to persecute Him would do the same to the disciples. So Jesus wanted every follower to know how to forgive.

In Matthew 5:39, Jesus spoke these challenging words to His disciples: "I tell you, do not resist an evil person. If anyone slaps you on the right cheek, turn to them the other cheek also." Jesus instructed them not to stop in the face of attack but to turn it around. Where the enemy wants his strike to stop you, instead let it grow you. Instead of fighting, forgive; rather than attack-ing, advance. Jesus knew there would be countless times when His disciples would have the opportunity to become sidelined by the enemy's strikes. He wanted them to know there is a response that the enemy cannot stop, and that is the turning power of forgiveness.

Turning the other cheek is not a sign of cowardice or weak-ness, as some may suggest, but it is a sign of strength and an ability to comprehend that God has not called you to fight every fight. He has only called you, as Paul told Timothy, to "fight the good fight of the faith" (1 Timothy 6:12). We need to learn how to turn the other cheek so that we can conserve our energy for the fights that really matter—the battles that will turn our world to our Savior, not away from Him.

Jesus knew His disciples would have to navigate not only external attacks but their own fallouts and disagreements as a team. He had called twelve to serve, as if they were one in heart and mind, which would mean they would need the willingness to forgive. Thomas's doubts were bound to offend Peter's faith; Judas would betray his Master, and the brothers James and John fought over who was the greatest. All these internal conflicts could have become huge distractions to the disciples' calling. Jesus needed His disciples to look past their personality differences and forgive. He knew time was short and their commission was vast. There was no room for their differences to become a distraction. Their ability to turn the other cheek would impact their effectiveness. Jesus wanted the disciples, in the face of hatred, to love; and in the places where there was no welcome, to keep moving. God wants the same resolve built into your life and mine.

Every time we allow our differences to shout louder than our commission as the body of Christ, our eyes are off the things we are called to turn around. We are to be an army that marches together. We are enlisted as brothers to fight against the injustices that seek to destroy people's lives. When we lose sight of the true fight to which we are all called, the enemy can cause us to take fire at the very people we need alongside us. We cannot afford to lose any person because of so-called friendly fire; we must forgive one another so that we can fight together.

> We must forgive one another so that we can fight together.

Too many Christians are missing in action; they have let offense take them out of the fight for which they were born. We must be willing to commit to what really matters. The enemy does not want your commitment to bring change or for you to find strength alongside other believers with the same cause. So he continues to seek to separate God's people, knowing if we draw lines around our differences we will become less effective. Yet when we allow forgiveness and grace to flow we discover something the enemy hates—we find a unity that is based not on personality but on purpose. Psalm 133:1–2 says, "How good and pleasant it is when God's people live together in unity! It is like precious oil poured on the head, running down." Unity is a powerful force among God's people. The power of unity can take a failing team to the top of their game or enable a united nation to win a war. The same is true in the spiritual realm: many spiritual battles are lost or won based on our ability to find the anointing that rests in unity. Untold productivity and peace abound when we find a way to come into agreement.

DIVERSITY NOT DISUNITY

When your natural body does not align correctly, it hinders your physical agility and strength. The same is true spiritually: the body of Christ must be aligned to honor one another. As the hands value the feet, the feet acknowledge the eyes, and they all work together for the common good of the body. Though our function in the body of Christ may differ, our purpose is the same. Forgiveness creates a flow to our function, allowing us to discover that diversity does not have to mean disunity.

Any parent with more than one child can tell you that each of their children has his or her own unique personality. It is the same with God's children. We are all His sons and daughters, yet we have different strengths, varying likes and dislikes. We see things from different perspectives and respond in unique ways to the situations we face. God does not want us to lose the characteristics that make us unique. He is calling for all His children to add their unique strengths to the turnaround mandate He has entrusted to His body.

As a mother, I am constantly teaching my children how their differences can become their greatest gift to each other. Our daughter loves to study and read, while our son prefers to be artistic and creative. When they combine these two strengths, they can produce some incredible results. And the same is true for God's people. If the spontaneous will work with the structured and the wild embrace the wise, then we create great strength rather than separation.

A TALE OF TWO BROTHERS

In Luke 15, we read a familiar parable of two brothers. These brothers served in their father's field together, yet each brother had a unique outlook on life. While the church has focused mostly on the younger brother who became the prodigal son, this story actually paints a picture of how our differences can become points of division.

These two brothers lived in the same house with their father, who loved them both. And they were both given the task of tending the land, which was their joint inheritance. Where the older brother was reliable, the younger was restless. Though their personalities were diverse, this fact did not need to cause them to divide. Their difference in approach could have been united to turn their field into a productive and lucrative business, yet this story tells a familiar tale of how the brothers failed to find the connection that could have held them together. When a time of testing came, the brothers drifted apart.

When the younger brother left home, he cut off all contact with his older brother and father, and his restlessness turned to recklessness as he partied and squandered all his inheritance. Meanwhile, his older brother moved from reliable to resentful as he deemed his younger brother unworthy of his place in his father's house. These two extremes of recklessness and resentment can be found in all areas of our lives, relationships, and workplaces; they are often the consequences of our failure to unite what the enemy wants to keep divided.

The restless brother held great potential. He had flair and creativity, and he had more ideas than hours in the day. Restless people are the ones who sit with their fingers twitching in the board meeting as their minds drift to all the things they could be doing. They want to explore, to try new things. They are not concerned with the budget, the paperwork, or meeting minutes that need to be fulfilled. The restless person sits across the table from his reliable brother, who is completely focused on the meeting's agenda and purpose. These two brothers can sit in the same room in many different scenarios in life, and too often their differences divide what God wants to unite.

Every time the enemy isolates these brothers, he takes what was made for strength and exposes it as weakness; he takes the restless one and gives him so much room that he becomes reckless. With no purpose to balance the passion and no roots to anchor his dreams, the restless brother becomes unproductive, and his restless nature can even lead to him becoming destructive, as was the case for the prodigal son. On the other hand, the isolated reliable brother can feel great resentment at all the hours he may be giving in comparison to the help he feels he is not receiving. His isolation exaggerates the burden of his work, and bitterness grows, as it did for the older brother who would not even come out to welcome his prodigal sibling home.

Too many times these brothers become strangers as their failure to speak each other's language separates what commitment and understanding could unite. And every time this separation takes place, we create more places where their reckless and resentful extremities can cause damage.

I have seen this parable played out too many times as churches have split, as generations have parted company when the restless failed to find a fit with the reliable, as the older brothers have judged and misunderstood the younger, as extroverts have marginalized the introverts, and as the rebellious have offended the religious. I have witnessed the restless entrepreneur partner with the reliable business investor—but though their different strengths could have been harnessed for great things, the partnership collapsed when they failed to find a way to communicate. I have watched families become distanced because a reliable parent cannot understand a restless child, and I have seen marriages end because what is reasonable to the restless spouse becomes dangerous to the reliable.

In this parable, God's heart is seen in the father who desires to have the brothers reconcile and find a way to strengthen and celebrate each other. Yet so often, just like in this parable, those whom God has called brothers we have made strangers. Our inability to forgive one another's failings has prevented us from seeing that though we may share different opinions, we belong to the same Father and are called by Him to work together in the same field. With every division, our power to turn things around is diminished, our voice is weakened, our time is wasted, and our testimony as God's family is becoming tarnished.

Throughout the Bible we find many scenarios where the strength of a turnaround has been undermined by the failure of God's people to forgive and turn the other cheek. From the very first family, whose relationship was fractured in the garden, emerged a brother who turned against brother. Jealousy and bitterness divided Cain and Abel (Genesis 4). Abel's reliability in bringing his best fat portion as an offering caused Cain to take the detour that offense offered him and led him to end his brother's life. When Cain asked God, "Am I my brother's keeper?" (v. 9), God's answer was the same then as it is today: *Yes.* We are all called to keep one another, brother to brother and sister to sister. We are called to be keepers of God's family. We are called to forgive the fractures our differences can cause and to hold together what hurt wants to pull apart. We are called to keep one another facing in the right direction so we can focus on the greater task to which we are called.

Cain's recklessness caused him to become known as a "restless wanderer," isolated and alone (v. 14). His life took a path that God had never intended; he was born to be a part of something so much bigger than a life of isolation could ever offer. This tale of separation runs throughout the Bible as brothers fail to be one another's keepers. Jacob lost his relationship with his brother, Esau, by stealing his birthright and deceiving him from his blessing. The twin brothers were separated from each other for years. David was not even invited to join his brothers when the prophet

Samuel came to anoint the next king. His brothers resented him even being on the same battlefield, where they were hiding from Goliath, yet David was anointed to deliver them from this giant.

We have to understand that this pattern of destruction and division wants to visit every generation. It wants to break every brotherhood bond that God has designed for strength and to set those who belong together against one another. The enemy wants to fracture God's family so that we are distracted by our own dysfunction and therefore of no help to the dysfunction in the world around us. These fractures can only be healed by forgiveness, which is why we must commit, however hard the stretch, to the turnaround power of a forgiving heart.

What Christian brother or sister are you missing? How has unforgiveness allowed you to become isolated from those you need the most? In what ways are you trying to turn around on your own things that we are destined to turn together? How much more could we achieve if we could seek to close every gap that our differences seek to create? God's people must find the forgiveness that pushes us forward even when our feelings want us to walk away.

REVENGE OR RESTORATION

Joseph's life also tells the story of the failure of brothers to be one another's keepers. Joseph was loved deeply by his aging father. However, his ten older brothers did not share the same affection for their younger sibling. They allowed the favor their father showed Joseph to feed a jealousy within their own hearts, and as a result, when their father asked them to watch over Joseph as he worked with them in the fields, they instead plotted to kill him. Joseph, who had neither sought to offend his brothers nor ever asked for his father's favor, now found himself isolated and ostracized from his own family.

Jealousy has the power to separate God's people. Often, our inability to celebrate one another's success has turned us from keepers to critics and turned friends to foes. Jealousy sabotages what grace covers. It exaggerates what forgiveness chooses to forget. Though Joseph was destined to save his brothers' lives, their jealousy convinced them to try to take his. How many times have we allowed jealousy to close our hearts to the vastness of God's plan? How many of the brothers we have deemed to be the problem has God intended to be part of our answer? We have to commit afresh to find the forgiveness that will ensure we see the turnaround in our generation that Joseph went on to make in his. In Genesis 37 we read that after years of separation Joseph reunited with his brothers. He had the opportunity and power in his role as prime minister of Egypt not only to show himself right to his brothers, but also to exact his revenge on them. Yet Joseph demonstrated the undeniable power of forgiveness when he chose to embrace his brothers, proving that even after years of separation, God can still bring reconciliation.

Even after years of separation, God can still bring reconciliation.

Joseph became a keeper of the brothers who tried to kill him. In Genesis 45 Joseph revealed his identity to his brothers and allowed forgiveness to flow. He embraced and wept over his brothers. He let the healing process start as he focused on their future and forgave their past. Joseph modeled for us in these moments the act of forgiveness. Forgiveness reconciles. It embraces. It removes the gap that bitterness creates and brings back together the relationships that God never intended to be separated. We, like Joseph, will be presented with many moments when we can let our words widen the gap or close it. We have a choice: Will we embrace or refrain from the moments that could bring brothers back together?

So often, in my journey, God has created moments where I have faced people and issues that have hurt and damaged me. I have the opportunity to close the gap or to remain distant. Sometimes I, like Joseph, have to choose to embrace instead of refrain; but at times I have found it extremely difficult to drop the pain in order to possess the promise. I have at times had to fast and pray until I could replace my hurt with God's healing power of forgiveness. I have had to wrestle my own feelings to make room for forgiveness. Forgiveness is not easy, and that is why conflicts and differences so often derail our progress in turning things around. Joseph, I am sure, fought with his feelings the day he recognized his brothers, but he allowed forgiveness to guide his steps. Forgiveness wants to guide you. It wants to unite and strengthen the family of God. It wants brothers and sisters to turn together and not against one another.

Joseph's mandate was to turn a nation; therefore, he had no time to turn against those whom he was called to help. Like Joseph, we must see the bigger gain over the temporary pain. We must accept that there will be times when our brothers mistreat us and times when we wrongly handle one other. We are all imperfect people, called to work together and to serve and seek after our perfect God, who models for us a forgiveness that covers rather than exposes, a forgiveness that embraces rather than refrains. We must call back every brother who has become isolated, and we must welcome every wanderer home. We need each member of the body of Christ to align together if we are going to turn the nations around.

We need each member of the body of Christ to align together if we are going to turn the nations around.

Where do you need to find this turnaround power in your life? Maybe for you it's time to make the turn found in repentance, or maybe you need to receive God's forgiveness. We all need to commit to the process of forgiving. Don't let your destiny come to a dead end. Let forgiveness turn your life around.

FIVE

MATURITY
MATTERS

IT WAS A SATURDAY AFTERNOON AND A GROUP OF NEIGHBORHOOD children had congregated in our kitchen. As they sat watching TV and chatting, I listened to their conversations. They talked excitedly of the adventures they were going to embark on that afternoon. The pirate ship they had created in our yard was about to come under attack after this short interval for juice and cookies. Their imaginations created a world of possibilities that made this ordinary Saturday afternoon an extraordinary day.

As they set out into the yard, the conversation rapidly changed to which role each person was going to play. Some were deemed worthy of the role of pirate, while the girls became mermaids and princesses. When all the roles were filled, each character headed out to the "high seas." After several hours of playing, tired from the sword fights and treasure hunts, the small group of friends went their separate ways, heading home for dinner and bed. Just like that, the game was over. There had been no fatalities, no permanent damage—just a lot of swashbuckling fun.

LET'S GET SERIOUS

As I watched this scenario play out, the Spirit of God reminded me that the adventure we are called to as His children is not an imaginary one. It is not a call to pretend for a few hours each weekend at church or to pretend with one another in our relationships. Just because we are considering changing our towns, cities, and neighborhoods and have a desire to see people saved, transformed, and restored does not mean this will happen, though this is the start. Unless we marry our desires with a partner called action, we are only playing pretend when it comes to turning around our communities. We are called to something that is much more serious. God has called us each to play our part in a real adventure. The fight we are called to engage in is very real—and our enemy is not playing games.

> God has called us each to play our part in a real adventure.

In 1 Peter 5:8 we are instructed to "be alert and of sober mind. Your enemy the devil prowls around like a roaring lion looking for someone to devour." The enemy is not messing around, nor is he merely threatening to bring harm. He is seeking people to devour and destroy. He is seeking those who are living unaware of his schemes, whose imaginary play has left them vulnerable in this very real battle. Their guard is down and they are potential prey for the enemy.

REALITY CHECK

God is not asking people to merely think about turning our world around; He is relying on us to do it. It's not just a nice thought for us to talk about or a potential adventure for us to consider embarking upon. God has enrolled us all in His commission; therefore, we have to stop pretending and get serious about the responsibility God asks us to carry.

Our society today is in danger of having many dreamers who are not real doers. All you have to do is flick through your TV channels to see countless programs where people have been told: "You can be the next greatest star if you just believe." You can watch thousands standing in line, waiting to audition for the latest pop music singing competition, hoping to find a shortcut to fame. While many in the line are hardworking musicians who deserve to be heard, they are always outnumbered by thousands of people with no musical background or practical experience in playing an instrument. These hopefuls are standing in line thinking they might stumble into an escape route to the celebrity life. They believe that just by showing up at the auditions, they will somehow end up a potential star. These imaginary contenders, much like the children in my backyard, are looking to play a role in a world they have dreamed up. Big dreams come crashing down for these aspiring artists, when after standing for a few hours in the cold, waiting for their big moment, they are stunned when one of the judges faces them with the reality of their lack of talent. Deflated and often emotionally volatile, they are forced to face facts and leave the room in which their dreams collided with reality.

As believers we need this experience where dreams face reality. As God's children, we are not called to stand in line, hoping for our own moment of greatness, or wait to become some spiritual superstar. There is no shortcut to God's turnaround. God does not give imaginary callings, nor does He play pretend. We need to enter God's reality room, not to be judged but to allow His Spirit to nudge us from our dream-state into a realization of what serving the turnaround God requires from each of us. We are not called to pretend-play the change; we are commissioned to *be* the change. Our lives are not about the end performance but about the discipline of daily practice. God is looking for those who will faithfully commit to developing their spiritual gifts and growing in faith. He is looking for those who will not waste time standing in a line but instead will invest a lifetime into helping needy lives.

> We are not called to pretend-play the change;
> we are commissioned to *be* the change.

God is looking not for once-a-week performers but for daily practitioners. He wants people who are taking what they have learned and passing on their wisdom, taking what has helped them grow and helping others to mature. We are not given gifts and talents so that we can entertain or impress one another but so that we can help the people whom others pass by. We need to position our lives and ministries so that the real challenges of this world shape the priorities of God's people. We must be ready to respond to the call of the broken, lost, and vulnerable. Our stage is our streets; our greatest gift is our acts of service.

Wherever God's people gather, we need to commit not merely to enjoying one another's company but to allowing our commission to shape our conversations and making the needs of others affect our choices. We need to talk about real problems and determine to play a real part in being an answer. When we see the full scale of what we are called to do, when we see the real reason we are called to turn things around, we will stop standing in line dreaming and instead start taking our turn and doing.

Let's consider those who have made biblical legendary status: Joseph the prime minister, David the giant killer, Daniel the lion tamer, Elijah the fire starter, Peter the rock, Solomon the wise, and many more. None of these men was a performer. They were never found wasting time in a line dreaming of being great. Instead, these men went to obscure places to be faithful, to serve diligently, and to commit to being a disciple of the difference they sought to see.

DISCIPLINED DREAMER

Joseph was labeled a dreamer by many, yet he did not live his life in a dreamlike state. When God gave him those dreams, Joseph didn't take that as permission to sit back and wait for his moment to arrive. If anything, Joseph's dreams brought him more harm than help at first. Joseph had to learn quickly that dreams require discipline. This future prime minister of Egypt did not enter Pharaoh's house demanding his potential be recognized; instead, he spent years working hard and serving faithfully, day in and day out. He endured wrongful accusations and imprisonment, yet throughout he stayed committed to being a man of integrity. He turned the prison around to such an extent that the prison warden trusted Joseph with the responsibility for all the other prisoners (Genesis 39:22).

Joseph turned around situations and people in every place he went. From the pit to the palace, he proved faithful and helped. Joseph took his dream and matched it with the discipline of dedication and diligence. He had a promise, but he also made a promise with his life that he would serve God and not stand in line waiting to be recognized.

FAITHFUL FOLLOWER

David didn't relax on a hill dreaming of his name in lights as the boy who would kill a giant. He was too busy taking care of his sheep, protecting them from the bear and lion, and doing his duties as errand-boy by taking food to his brothers in battle. His faithfulness meant that not only did he deliver sandwiches, but he also served up Goliath's head on the side. David was not trying to be famous; he was simply being faithful. His story is not an imaginary tale; it is an account of what happens when we stop waiting and we start participating in God's work of turning things around.

Proverbs 12:11 says, "Those who work their land will have abundant food, but those who chase fantasies have no sense."

We must ensure that we do not build a faith that is more fantasy than reality. We have the wisdom to know the difference between dreaming and doing, between chasing and trusting. Wherever people and places have been abandoned, God wants to send His people to bring abundance. But the only way that this can happen is through our commitment to embrace the process of turning, including all the work and demand it will bring into our lives.

God needs a discerning people who can say no to pursuing the things that become a distraction and yes to the disciplines that will change an environment. Maturity chooses to accept the work that change requires; it is not afraid of the commitment or investment. Where the immature want to leave early and pay later, the mature are willing to pay in advance for the change they seek to see. Maturity does not place short-term gain over achieving lifelong improvements.

> Maturity does not place short-term gain
> over achieving lifelong improvements.

GROWING INTO IT

One of my favorite relationships in the Bible is the apostle Paul's mentoring of his disciple Timothy. Timothy was a young man who had great opportunities ahead of him. Paul wanted to ensure that Timothy was not just called to ministry but also prepared for the work that ministry requires. On many occasions I have heard young people quote these words of Paul to Timothy as they want people to respect them and listen to what they have to say: "Don't let anyone look down on you because you are young" (1 Timothy 4:12). But this line was not the end of Paul's wisdom for Timothy; Paul goes on to give him a great deal more wisdom. Paul was not instructing his young student to demand people's respect. He was instructing Timothy how to live so that his life would be worthy of people's respect.

Paul went on to say, "Don't let anyone look down on you because you are young, but set an example in speech, in conduct, in love, in faith and in purity. Until I come, devote yourself to the public reading of Scripture, to preaching and to teaching. Do not neglect your gift. . . . Be diligent in these matters; give yourself wholly to them, so that everyone may see your progress" (vv. 12–15).

This truth is timeless. It is not just wisdom that Paul was dispensing for the spiritually young, but it is a truth to which we all have to constantly commit. All advancement is dependent on our investment, and there have been many times when my willingness to become disciplined has determined the strength of my voice and witness as a wife, mother, and leader.

> All advancement is dependent on our investment.

THE COST

The apostle Paul was describing for Timothy what it costs to be a leader of God's people. In his call to turn around the early church, Paul had endured great hardships that he wanted to prepare his younger student for. Paul did not use his time with Timothy to speak of his many great achievements; instead, he went to great lengths to teach him the lessons he would need to learn to sustain him in every test his turnaround call would bring. Paul told Timothy that if you want people to look up to you, then you must commit to growing yourself. Paul was letting him know that this was not playtime but the time to practice. Paul did not want Timothy to teach a message he hadn't first lived himself.

The same is true with God and His people today. He doesn't want His people trying to turn things around that they have not committed to turn around in themselves. It's time for each of us to commit to the ongoing call to grow up and to hear the voice of God asking us to set an example. Paul was asking Timothy to turn his speech around and to line up his confession with his convictions. He was asking him to work on his faith, purity, and love. We cannot ask a world to turn to God when our lives are still full of compromise. We cannot ask those whose lives are away from God to purify themselves when those who know God are not seeking a life of purification. Timothy was not expected to be perfect. He was being asked to be a practitioner of the turnaround he was called to bring before he became a preacher of those changes to others.

> It's time for each of us to commit to the ongoing call to grow up and to hear the voice of God asking us to set an example.

TIME TO LEAVE THE NURSERY

When my children were younger, one of their favorite films was *Peter Pan* (and the truth is, it's still one of mine!). On one occasion, we were watching this film as we had many times before, and on this particular day I felt God's Spirit speak to my own heart. The scene that was unfolding was where the young girl, Wendy, is playing in the nursery and her father comes in to tell her it is time for her to stop acting so childish because she is getting older. Her father announced that this would be her last night in the nursery, as tomorrow it would be time to grow up. The scene changed, and as Wendy is contemplating her father's words, through the window comes Peter Pan with a very different proposal. He sees Wendy's moment of indecision and extends his hand with the words, "Wendy, don't listen to your father. Come with me to a place where you never, ever have to grow up and where you can stay a child forever. Come with me to Neverland." In that moment, I felt God whisper to my spirit, *My people must decide. I am their Father asking them to leave the nursery, but many would rather stay in Neverland.*

Neverland is a place where nothing is real. There is no work, no pain, and no responsibilities. It was a place for lost boys. We can create this same utopia in our world today. We can believe that it's okay to stay immature, to never forgive, to never take responsibility, and to never commit. But if we stay in Neverland, the nations will never turn to their Savior. Instead, we will increase the population of lost boys—boys who will never know they have a Father who is calling them home.

Like Wendy's father, God wants us to trust His words. Though they may seem less exciting than Peter Pan's, they are words that will graduate us from the nursery level in God to the arenas to take on the giants. God needs us to hear His voice saying, *It's time to grow up.* There are some very grown-up responsibilities we are destined to help turn around. There are some daunting realities we are the answer to, but we cannot address these realities from the nursery.

Neverland living prevents your life from finding its true capacity and depth. If we never step out, we never develop our faith. If we never commit, we fail to find the joy and reward of completion. Too many times our habitation of Neverland has held us back from the true adventure of faith.

THE GROWTH LIMITATION

If we fail to grow up in God, we will limit what God is able to reveal and entrust to us. Just as you wouldn't ask a five-year-old to run your home, God wouldn't ask immature followers to turn around His precious world. He is searching for those who will put in the work to grow so that He can send them to the places where His Spirit is longing for His people to go.

The writer of Hebrews felt he was unable to share with God's people the wisdom he knew God had for them. He felt bound by their immaturity, and so what he was able to teach them was less than what God wanted them to have. Due to his frustration with the childish arguments in the church at that time, he called the church to grow up:

> We have much to say about this, but it is hard to make it clear to you because you no longer try to understand. In fact, though by this time you ought to be teachers, you need someone to teach you the elementary truths of God's word all over again. You need milk, not solid food! Anyone who lives on milk, being still an infant, is not acquainted with the teaching

about righteousness. But solid food is for the mature, who by constant use have trained themselves to distinguish good from evil. (Hebrews 5:11–14)

When our local church has traveled into the darkest part of our city, we have found that the enemy is not playing a game. He is ready to fight to keep the territory he has turned into a dark place. We cannot show up unprepared and immature to face the enemy's schemes. We have to be mature in our faith and in our ability to wage war with the Word of God. We have to enter strengthened by the solid food of our faith. God's turnarounds require us to graduate from milk to solid food. What is acceptable when you are a child is inappropriate when you are older. We have to grow up and sign up to the work this turnaround calling requires.

HEIGHT RESTRICTIONS

For some, the thought of growing up seems very unappealing. It sounds like all work and no play. It sounds more exhausting than enjoyable. However, the truth is that growing up does not mean God is calling us to a life of no fun; it just means that the fun changes. If you have ever been to an amusement park, you know that the best rides and most adventurous roller coasters have a height restriction. They have deemed this certain kind of fun is only appropriate for those who have grown up to a certain height. The restriction is not there to prevent you from having fun; it's there to make sure that the level of fun is something the rider can handle.

We recently went to Disney World, and several friends told me that I needed to ride the Tower of Terror. I like roller coasters, but I was not so sure about this one. After much persuasion, I agreed to give the ride a go. As I went to get in line, our younger child, who was only three at the time, insisted that he was coming with me. He seemed to think this ride looked a lot like one of the other rides he enjoyed. After trying to convince him this was not going to be fun, I calmed him down and agreed with my husband that I would carry him as far as the entrance to the ride and then give the Disney staff member the task of explaining to my son that he was too young to go on the ride. I was convinced when he reached their measuring checkpoint my three-year-old wouldn't make the height requirement so the staff member would inform him of the bad news. To my shock and my son's delight, when we arrived at the measuring bar, my son, who is very tall for his age, just fit on the line and access was granted. I went into panic mode, knowing he would hate every second of this ride; yet I couldn't talk him out it. So we entered the ride together. Five seconds in, the doors were locked and the lights went out and all anyone could hear was my three-year-old screaming, "Mummy, get me off this ride!" Of course there was no turning back. I will always remember how the Tower of Terror lived up to its name for my son.

God knows what spiritual height we need to be at to take on some of the adventures He has for us. David committed to growing up, and in doing so, he graduated to giant killing. Daniel devoted himself and graduated to lion taming. Joseph grew up and graduated to nation leading. Growing up is not boring. If anything, it's a guarantee that God will use your life in more adventures. The risks will increase as your faith grows.

GROW UP, NOT OLD

So how do we grow up? How do we know if our lives are growing like God wants them to grow? Just as Paul advised Timothy, we must commit to the same disciplines of devoting ourselves to the work of growth. Growth will not just happen, and maturity is not inevitable. We can hear the words "grow up" as "grow old." We can misinterpret the need to work on growing up. Eventual age does not necessarily mean that we will also grow up. I have met many older people who are still very immature. Growing old is inevitable, but growing up is a choice. The more we neglect the call to grow up, the more immature believers we produce and the fewer workers we have available for the grown-up job of turning our communities and world around.

| Growing old is inevitable, but growing up is a choice. |

If you are serious about turning things around, then you need to get a growth plan for your life. We need to shape up and take on the work we are called to carry out. Just as in the natural your physical body has to work out to bear weight, so must your spiritual body. Paul gave Timothy a growth plan and he told him to work on these areas. Let's consider those areas here as a growth plan for our own lives.

DEVOTE YOURSELF

Paul asked Timothy to become devoted in the areas to which he was called to bring direction. He instructed, "Until I come, devote yourself to the public reading of Scripture, to preaching and to teaching" (1 Timothy 4:13). He didn't want Timothy teaching something he had not lived. God needs us to find the same place of devotion. He wants our private world to match our public words. Timothy had to grow through application of the Word of God, through the daily discipline of prayer, and through understanding God's ways.

God is looking for your life to have a growth plan that is not dependent on another person's devotion but that is able to grow because of your own desire to learn. Paul did not want to be the growth plan for Timothy; he knew he couldn't be there to keep Timothy strong. He would be away when Timothy faced testing times and challenges. Paul wanted Timothy's own devotion to hold him fast. We often fail to grow because we base our growth pattern on those around us. We rely on the devotion of our peers or leaders, and we feed off what they have found in the Word as food for our life. We have to take the responsibility to be self-feeders. Just as a baby requires another to give it food, when we rely on the devotion of others, we remain infantile in our growth pattern. We then only grow when they are willing to feed us.

Maturity means preparing your own food by digging into the Word and uncovering truth that can shape your life. Where do you need to be more devoted? Is it to His Word, to prayer, to serving, to committing? The ability you have to devote yourself will impact your speed and ability to grow in season and out. God needs us to be able to take on responsibilities that we are willing and devoted to carry through. We cannot let our devotion become dependent on our feelings or our circumstances. If our devotion depends on our feelings or emotions, we will quit before we ever see the turnaround God has in mind for us.

It was Daniel's devotion to prayer that made him refuse to forsake his prayers to God. It was David's devotion to service that kept him following when others quit. It was Paul's devotion to the Word that caused him to preach in prison and in front of key politicians. It is our devotion to God that will grow our lives, not God's devotion to us. He is devoted to us no matter what, but we must grow our devotion so that we, too, can stand firm when the less devoted want to sit down.

NEVER NEGLECT

Every one of us has been given a spiritual gift. It was woven into our lives at conception. God gave you an ability to turn things around, whether it be through service, wisdom in the Word, or the ability to lead. Paul urges us, "Do not neglect your gift" (1 Timothy 4:14). We must nurture our spiritual gifts because all gifts are of value; God will use whatever gift you have. I have observed how a person's gift of hospitality can turn the hardest of hearts toward God. I have seen the gift of songwriting unlock lives that have been shut down. God will use whatever gift He has given you to demonstrate His turning power. Each gift's strength depends on our willingness to invest and grow it. Just as a roaring fire can be reduced to dying embers through neglect, so it is with the gifts in our lives. We decide the temperature of the heat generated by our gifts through the commitment and time we put into them.

> God will use whatever gift He has given you to demonstrate His turning power.

When I was fourteen years old, someone spoke something into my life that at the time seemed quite unrealistic. This person envisioned me speaking to many lives, being a teacher of the Word, being strong and taking on many challenges for God. To a teenage girl with no apparent desire for ministry, that seemed a mistake. But I remember that after receiving what the person had said, I read 1 Timothy 4:14 and felt God give me the same advice as Paul gave Timothy. I felt challenged that even though I didn't understand all God was asking from me, I felt the responsibility to tend to my gift and to not neglect it. I began to practice my gift of speaking. At first, I spoke to a few unimpressed horses in a field near my home, but later to some friends and eventually, a larger group. The places I spoke changed, but the commitment to not neglect my gift held fast.

What spiritual gift are you neglecting that God wants to use in His turning? What seedling with the potential to grow into a strong sapling and become a source of great harvest have you failed to water? Sometimes because we see no use for our gift, we tell ourselves it is not worth the investment. At age fourteen, no one was asking me to speak, but God was asking me to water a seed. We have to start where we can in order to tend to the gift and fan it into flame.

Your gift is unique; it's your job to steward the seed you have. No one else can sow for you and, therefore, we must look again at what we have been entrusted with and give it the attention it deserves. What can you start doing today, as part of your growth plan, to make sure your gift is ready and strong enough to help in God's great turnarounds?

BE DILIGENT

Diligence is a key word for any growth plan. Your devotion will only be as successful as your diligence to it. Your gift will only grow as you commit to diligently tending to it. Diligence is a mature word; it asks for accountability and reliability.

The apostle Paul said, "Be diligent in these matters; give yourself wholly to them, so that everyone may see your progress. Watch your life and doctrine closely. Persevere in them, because if you do, you will save both yourself and your hearers" (1 Timothy 4:15–16). Paul was asking Timothy to give himself wholeheartedly and regularly, not in a one-off grand statement of commitment, but with a consistent commitment to preserve his growth ethic. Often the difference between those who make a difference and those who imagine they are called to make a difference is the word *diligence*. It's the commitment to show up even when no one else will. It's the study no one sees and the sacrifice no one applauds. It's David's diligence on a hillside to protect a few sheep when no one else is looking. It's the diligence shown by Joseph in prison to be a faithful steward when no one expects it.

> Often the difference between those who make a difference and those who imagine they are called to make a difference is the word *diligence*.

Our community does not need God's people to charge in like knights in shining armor. They don't need promises that are never going to be kept or commitments that are never seen through to completion. God's turnarounds require those who understand what it is to persevere and to be diligent. In our city, we have been involved helping the street girls for over ten years. The reason that their lives are being turned around is not because we impressed them with our gospel presentation or that we quoted our best messages to them. The reason they want God to turn their lives around is because we have diligently turned up. Diligence is a language the enemy hates. He can't throw diligent people off their cause with a few problems because they have developed a perseverance that will keep them turning up. Paul knew Timothy had a call on his life to turn people to Christ, and he wanted Timothy's commitment to reach maturity so that his diligence would forge in him a deep determination to see the job for which he was sent completed.

The reason they want God to turn their lives around is because we have diligently turned up.

God is looking to you and me to grow up and to progress from the flight simulator of Christianity into the real work we are called to do. God's turnarounds require His people not just to show up, but to grow up and to mature. There are many risks out there that we will need to embrace, but God is waiting for you and me to get to the height they require.

SIX

OWN YOUR ZONE

ULTIMATELY OUR ABILITY TO TURN ANYTHING AROUND depends on our willingness to accept our responsibility for the changes that need to be made. Just as a child walks away from the mess in a kitchen thinking, *It's not my responsibility*, we as adults have to challenge any remnants of this same thinking. We have to ask ourselves, "Do I feel responsible for the things that are out of order around me? Are they my responsibility or do I defer this task to someone else?" Eventually you have to identify what "your zone" is that God is looking to you to "own."

SLEEPING ON THE JOB

Proverbs 24:30–34 says, "I went past the field of a sluggard, past the vineyard of someone who has no sense; thorns had come up everywhere, the ground was covered with weeds, and the stone wall was in ruins. I applied my heart to what I observed and learned a lesson from what I saw: A little sleep, a little slumber, a little folding of the hands to rest—and poverty will come on you like a thief and scarcity like an armed man."

This man was entrusted with a place of potential that God wanted him to transform. He was given a place that could have produced grapes, thus creating a source of revenue through the vineyard for his future. However, where there could have been vines, he had thorns; in place of wheat were weeds; and instead of resources from his vineyard, he was contending with ruins. This man had fallen asleep on his God-assigned patch. Though he was entrusted with this space, he did not take responsibility for it—and the same picture could be seen in many of our lives. God has also given each of us a field, a place to grow and flourish. We have been entrusted with a place to call home, relationships, friends and family, places to work, and communities to dwell in. Each of us has a field to take care of, and we all have a God-given responsibly to nurture it into the most productive space we can.

TURN THE SOIL

"Look at this, Mum!" came the cry from my daughter's bedroom. I went to see what all the excitement was about and found our daughter, Hope Cherish, perched on her bedroom window-sill, eyes wide open in wonder, looking down at our neighbors' newly renovated backyard. While I had been aware they were doing some landscaping next door, I hadn't realized the full extent of the makeover.

My daughter wanted me to see the finished result from her bird's-eye vantage point. She pointed at the garden and began to describe all of the incredible features, from the stream that ran all the way through the backyard, to the hot tub and sauna in the far corner, to the little bridge perfect for children to walk across, to the beautifully landscaped borders. She was right; it was stunning. We paused while we took it all in and then came the inevitable question: "Mum, why doesn't our garden look like that?" Yes, it was true: our garden bore no resemblance at all to our neighbors'. Though not unkempt, our yard now looked dull and neglected in comparison.

As I was preparing to give her some lengthy reasons for why this was, she answered her own question: "I guess it's because you and Dad never do any gardening." And with that statement, suddenly all my planned answers were shown for what they really were—excuses! My daughter had identified in that one observation the root of the problem: although Steve and I loved to be in the garden, we didn't love working in it. When our neighbors had taken the time to turn the soil and irrigate the land, we had wasted time complaining about how much work needed to be done and how hard the soil conditions were. While we were talking about how beautiful our garden could potentially be, our neighbors had turned the talk into action and were now enjoying the great view we desired. Our soil was the same, and the seeds they planted were widely available. But our attitude was the difference. While Steve and I were talking about why it couldn't happen, our neighbors had made it happen. They had turned their yard around.

SPACE ENVY

So often we can get space envy. Like my daughter, Hope, we can spend our days peering into other people's lives, ministries, and businesses, longingly looking at all the vegetation, growth, and beauty; then contrast that with our own lives and begin to formulate our excuses for why our fields don't look as good as theirs. While we all have a different context in which we are doing life, we serve the same God and have the same Word and promises extended to all our lives. Our neighbors' yard had the same soil as ours, we shared the same sunlight and rainfall, and we both had the same amount of hours in a day. So the difference in our yards' appearances was not due to conditions outside of our control. They had not let their busy lifestyle or fair-weather excuses keep them from the hard work the turnaround would require. They had simply done something that we had not: they looked at that backyard and committed to taking responsibility for the ground within their boundary lines. In doing so, they awakened the soil's potential and turned a barren space into a flourishing oasis.

> While we all have a different context in which we are doing life, we serve the same God and have the same Word and promises extended to all our lives.

If you were to look close enough at that flourishing ministry, marriage, or business you have been peering over the fence of your life to admire, I guarantee you would also find the same truth—inside that space, someone took what he was given and decided to turn the soil to make the most of what he had been entrusted with. He denied himself the temptation of slumber and refused to fold his arms; instead, he dug deep and pulled weeds to find the beauty underneath the bleak landscape.

Many times we pray to God to tend our gardens for us, but from the beginning of creation when God placed Adam and Eve into the garden, He instructed them to work the land and take ownership of it: "The LORD God took the man and put him in the Garden of Eden to work it and take care of it" (Genesis 2:15). God could have designed creation so that it tended itself. He could have controlled what was planted and determined what would flourish. But God was not going to be humanity's heavenly groundskeeper; He was building a work ethic into his relationship with Adam and Eve, and He was placing into humans' hands a mandate to take responsibility for the place in which He had purposed they would dwell and build their lives. He gave men and women the power to rule and bring order, and the skills to cultivate and produce great fruit from the land. God didn't want His children dependent on handouts: He wanted them to exercise their ability to work hard and reap the rewards.

We cannot pray to God to come and take care of a space He has entrusted to us; God wants to bless the fruits of our labor, not do the labor for us. God is looking at our lives as He did Adam's and Eve's—positioned by heaven to bring His life and bounty into the soil's barrenness. God is looking for His people to work their land and to turn their soil around so that every space can reflect His goodness and glory.

INVEST IN YOUR ZONE

So what about our fields? Proverbs 24 says the sluggard had been given a field to look after and God was holding him accountable for that space. God has designed all of our lives so that we, too, are accountable for fields. Let's call them *zones*—areas we have been entrusted with, places where we live, relationships we share, and gifts and talents we have been given. Each of us has a zone. God will not ask you about other people's zones; He does not demand from our lives fruit we cannot produce. He knows exactly where we are positioned and what potential is within us, and it is in those areas of potential that God asks us to arise and "own our zone."

In Matthew 25:14–30, Jesus tells a parable of a landowner who entrusted his servants with gold to invest while he went away. On his return the master asked to see what each servant had achieved with the gold he had been given. While two were praised for doubling their money, the third was chastised because instead of increasing the value of his gold, the servant had buried his money to keep it safe. In response to this servant's failure to make an investment, the master became angry and took away this man's bag of gold and handed it to the one who had made the highest return.

This parable could seem unfair; the master could be seen as unkind. Yet Jesus painted this picture to remind God's servants everywhere that they, too, have a responsibility to bring a return off the life they have been entrusted with. God does not want us to hide our abilities for fear we may fail or ignore our gifts because of our lack of confidence. He is looking for us to overcome our nerves and produce a harvest from our lives. Where two men in this parable owned their zones and doubled their investments, another lost all the potential that was possible.

In the backyard at our home, we had some areas that looked better than others. We had turned our front entrance, for example, into a beautiful canopy of hanging baskets and candle lights, but it got less impressive the farther you ventured into the yard. I had invested in some parts of my yard and not others, yet they were all in my zone. We have to be careful we don't allow the same imbalance to happen in our lives, perfecting our professional "front" while we have left the back door wide open for dysfunction and compromise to enter.

God wants each of us to commit every part of our zones to line up with His Word and promises. From our beliefs to our behavior, we should have a consistent willingness to own each zone of our lives until it is flourishing. We need to take an inventory of all that God has placed in our zones: all the places where we are doing life, all the people we are connected to, where we live, the streets around our home, the gifts in our lives, the places of work or study where we are situated. Whatever your zone consists of, are you willing to take responsibility for it? Will you confront where things are being handled carelessly and reclaim the places that have become neglected?

Whatever your zone consists of, are you willing to take responsibility for it?

ATTACK APATHY

In order to "own our zone," we must attack the killer called apathy. This deadly disease often enters our zones gradually, like a tranquilizer; over time it can put to sleep the biggest of dreams and the most ambitious of plans. Apathy is a slow-seeping sedative that calms our passion and quiets our quest. The sluggard in Proverbs 24 allowed apathy to enter his zone. Weeds grew and walls collapsed, but not because of adverse weather or an attack by vandals. No, the perpetrator of this demise was the owner of the field who made an error in judgment and chose "a little sleep, a little slumber, a little folding of the arms to rest" when he should have been working his land (Proverbs 24:33).

Apathy is a slow-seeping sedative that calms our passion and quiets our quest.

It doesn't take much for apathy to attack; you don't have to be asleep for very long for a lot of things to go wrong. This man was not in hibernation; he was just napping. It was only "a little slumber." But in those few moments when his eyes were closed and his hands were folded, the enemy was wide awake and ready to go. I believe apathy is one of the greatest weapons in the enemy's arsenal. He would rather take on a sleepy sluggard over a wide-awake warrior any day. Too often, we have looked for the enemy in all the wrong places. We are looking for the obvious, when he is often far subtler. Instead of bringing you a nightmare, he will sometimes sing you a lullaby. He will happily rock you to sleep knowing that your apathy can become his doorway of opportunity.

Have you noticed how we can often start something with much more strength than with which we finish, if we even finish at all? The enthusiasm we had when we embarked on that new opportunity, relationship, or ministry can quickly fade away if we don't strengthen it proactively. Once we begin, we can become overwhelmed with the amount of work this venture requires. It is in the middle of our involvement that we are the highest potential as a target for an apathy attack. It's then when we can entertain thoughts that before we would have never given the time of day to. We wonder, "Does it matter?" or, "Is it worth the effort?" And as we relax our resolve, we start to doubt our dreams. Then as we let down our guard, the enemy steps up his game.

Apathy is all too often the reason that great ideas never get realized and some of the most amazing turnarounds never transpire. We walk off the job, never attaining the prize, when we are called to own our zone and take the turn. We must become skilled at identifying when apathy is about to attack so we can fight back with determination to finish what we started.

I remember once running an outreach project in a particularly needy part of our town. We had a team that very enthusiastically offered to go and serve in the community center to help bring a turnaround in the lives of the young people who went there. When our team showed up, they did not receive the welcome they had expected from the young people. No one expressed a desire to receive help or even make any connection with our willing volunteers. When we asked why these young people were so resistant to our arrival, the community center's staff explained how we were the third Christian organization that had showed up to help, but up until now, not one of them had followed through on the commitment they had made. The teenagers had been more difficult than they had anticipated and the conditions far from perfect, so the people who had made all the promises began to make excuses. They had started with the aim to transform that community and turn around troubled teenagers' lives, but as the weeks went by they had become less enthusiastic and indifferent toward things they had said they would make a difference in. Apathy had attacked their spirits, and instead of bringing a turnaround, they let their apathy turn them away. Apathy cannot turn a city; it can't shape a community, grow a ministry, or impact our world. Apathy puts on its slippers where passion used to put on sneakers. Apathy lets things go that God has asked us to own. Apathy says it doesn't matter when your spirit knows it does. The apathy that begins to creep into your life is the beginning of you losing control of your zone.

> Apathy puts on its slippers where passion used to put on sneakers.

TAKE AUTHORITY

The cure for apathy is found when we take our authority in Christ. So often, we put up with compromise because we are uncomfortable to confront it. We let apathy convince us we have no power to change things, when the reality is that we have the power in Him to change everything. We have the power to bring order to chaos, to speak to the storm, to turn confusion to clarity and brokenness to wholeness. Through Christ, we have in our lives the power to bring change. Taking our authority in Christ and putting it to use is not about a power trip or permission to become a control freak. Rather, it is about being aware that we have been given an authority that we are responsible for stewarding wisely.

Through Christ, we have in our lives the power to bring change.

The plan of heaven is that God's will be done here on earth, and for that to happen, we have to stop letting apathy allow us to abdicate our turns. Jesus taught His disciples how to own their zones. He knew He was not going to be there for the disciples every day to help them navigate the crowds and the cries for help; He couldn't go to every lame person and teach every searching heart. Jesus wanted the disciples to own their time, towns, and responsibilities. He wanted to ensure they understood the authority they were being given. Jesus didn't call the disciples to live in isolated space away from the maddening crowd; He wanted them to be sent out with the knowledge that they were empowered to turn their world around.

Matthew 10:1 says, "Jesus called his twelve disciples to him and gave them authority to drive out impure spirits and to heal every disease and sickness." Then Jesus, after calling them in, sent them out to take authority and turn lives around. He said, "As you go, proclaim this message: 'The kingdom of heaven has come near.' Heal the sick, raise the dead, cleanse those who have leprosy, drive out demons" (vv. 7–8).

This was no small list of things Jesus was asking them to do. They weren't being sent on an evangelistic holiday. Jesus was sending them to kick the Devil out of lives he had terrorized for years and to take back the ground he had stolen from God's people. The disciples were expected to take the authority He had given them and put it to use.

Today, God is expecting the same of His modern-day disciples. He is sending us out to bring His life to our towns and cities. But, just as with the twelve disciples, He is not sending us out ill equipped. He has given us authority that we have to learn to exercise and use. We may feel powerless when we look at the needs around us, but the truth is we have God's power. God does not ask us to turn things around without providing us with the authority to do it. He is not going to send you into a battle without a weapon or into enemy territory without His higher authority. God wants to equip us; we just have to commit to use His equipping well.

> God does not ask us to turn things around without providing us with the authority to do it.

MOUNTAIN MOVE

The disciples knew they had been given power and authority. They had exercised it and watched how when they spoke the word, miracles would happen. But later on, in Matthew 17, we see Jesus confronting the disciples over their inability to deliver a troubled boy using the authority He had given them. The boy's father came to Jesus, begging him to remove the torment-ing spirit from his young son because the disciples had failed to take authority over the demon. Even though the disciples had delivered people from demonic possession on previous occa-sions, they failed to turn this situation around. When they asked Jesus why they had failed, His reply was a sharp reminder to the disciples that the power hadn't changed but that apathy had attacked: "You have so little faith. Truly I tell you, if you have faith as small as a mustard seed, you can say to this mountain, 'Move from here to there,' and it will move. Nothing will be impossible for you" (Matthew 17:20).

Jesus' famous statement about the mustard seed has been quoted many times, yet how many times have we truly believed it? Do we really believe and exercise the authority we have been given? Are we confident that when we speak it out, we will move any mountains in our zones?

Do we really believe and exercise the authority we have been given?

If you have ever spent any time in a mountain range, you will know just how impressive and awesome they can be. I have had the privilege of viewing several mountain ranges in many nations of the world. From the polar-capped mountains of Switzerland to the dusty mountaintops in the desert, each mountain strikes its own impressive silhouette across all those who come to survey it.

On one occasion I was in Cape Town when the opportunity presented itself for me to climb Table Mountain. I had climbed hills before but never a mountain, so I was keen to accept the challenge. In the searing heat, some friends and I began our ascent. It took hours of hard climbing until eventually, tired and aching, we reached the top. As we got to the summit of the mountain, there was the strangest sight, for as we reached the top, sweating and exhausted, we came around the corner to find people walking past us in heels and business suits. They had caught the cable car up to the mountaintop and were booked for lunch in one of the air-conditioned mountaintop cafés. I remembered, after witnessing this contrast, this scripture about mountain-moving faith. So many of the mountains we are precariously trying to climb, God has a cable car for. He has a way to move the obstacles that no one else can seem to move. Where we may be barely hanging on, He is ready to carry us.

In every mountain we face, God wants to give us mountain-moving assistance. He wants our faith to be exercised and our prayer life to be intensified. Sometimes it is easier to just clamber up our mountains; we would rather try to scrape our way through than put our faith on the line. Yet we need to find the confidence to speak to the things that have overshadowed our lives for too long. Maybe you are facing a mountain of debt, a mountain of stress, or mounting sickness in your body. We have to learn as God's people how to access spiritually the cable car called faith that helps us remove the intimidation of the mountain and reach the summit sooner.

> In every mountain we face, God wants to give us mountain-moving assistance.

IS THAT IT?

The disciples had forgotten the power they had within them, and they let a demon take the ground God had given them. They needed reminding that the authority given to them was based not on who they were but on Whose they were, and we also need to constantly be reminded of the same truth. The Devil may think he has rights in your life, but he has none. Christ paid for you to have freedom, to be fruitful, and to turn your world around. So don't let the enemy turn down your volume. Just as Jesus reminded the disciples, "Nothing will be impossible for you," maybe you need to remind yourself of that truth today. You need to shout His name over your zone until you see mountains move.

> You need to shout His name over your zone until you see mountains move.

I learned this lesson firsthand when my son suddenly fell sick one evening. It was the night before our family took a much-needed break, and as we had just finished packing bags, suddenly my son started to feel faint; he was running a fever and got very sick. My husband and I had started to notice a pattern with our family: whenever we were about to do something to replenish our lives and re-energize for all we were called to do, someone would suddenly become attacked with illness, thus ruining the much-needed break. So true to form, out of nowhere, Noah's sickness become rapidly worse. I put Noah to bed and began to make all the rearrangements in my head for what looked like yet another postponed trip. It was later that night when I went in to check on Noah as he lay sleeping that I quietly prayed over him.

I walked out of his bedroom and felt God speak strongly into my spirit, *Is that it?*

"Is that what, Lord?" was my reply.

Is that all you are going to do about this situation?

I examined my short and rather apathetic prayer I had just prayed and felt God stir up my spirit that it was time to own my zone and take my authority.

This was my son who was ill, in our house. This was our vacation that was going to be ruined, and I did not want my apathy to allow this illness to go unchallenged. I promptly turned around and walked back into our son's room. This mama bear had just come out of hibernation and I was mad. Mad at the enemy for being in my zone, and mad at the apathy I had let attack my spirit. As Noah lay there fast asleep, I began to pace his bedroom floor and own my zone. I declared health to his sick body and spoke the Word over him. I told the enemy to stop squatting in my space and attacked the apathy with my God-given authority.

As I brought my prayer to a close, I said, "In the name of Jesus . . . ," and what happened next completely freaked me out, as from his deep sleep my son shouted, "Amen!" I looked at Noah, who was still fast asleep, eyes closed and not moving, and said again, "In the name of Jesus . . . ," and again he shouted back at me, "Amen!" The power of God hit my son and me that night, and I realized that even though my son's body was asleep, his spirit was wide awake and clearly thrilled that his mom had just woken up.

I came out of the room crying and shaking under the power of God as I related to my husband what had just happened. I told him that I wasn't going to take "a little slumber" on my spiritual watch. I understood again that night that God had given me authority and permission to use this spiritual authority any time I wanted to turn things around. That night, not only did my son's health turn around and sickness leave, but something inside my heart turned around as I committed afresh to own my zone.

There are so many things in the zones we own, as individuals and as families, about which God is saying, *Any time you want, you can turn this around.* From our marriages to our ministries, we don't have to put up with things Christ has already paid the price for. What compromise has moved in that you need to move out? Why are you living with just enough when you serve the God of more than enough? The weeds you have learned to live with need to be uprooted, because in their place you can plant new seeds and find new productivity.

> Why are you living with just enough when you serve the God of more than enough?

Where do you need to walk back through the door of your zone with a new perspective and a new determination to turn things around? We have to get passionate about this if we are going to bring change. Jesus' passion for people wouldn't allow Him to walk past the hurting or ignore the dying. When He entered a zone, things turned around.

ZEAL FOR YOUR HOUSE CONSUMES ME

In John 2, Jesus entered the temple, a place where people would go to bring their offerings and worship to God. As Jesus entered, He found that apathy had attacked inside His Father's house and many compromises had been made. In the place where people should have been coming to sacrifice, traders were selling their goods; where people should have been worshipping, money was being exchanged for excessive profit.

When Jesus saw this, His response was not gentle. He didn't suggest that people leave; He entered that zone and owned it, and He began to literally turn things around. "In the temple courts he found people selling cattle, sheep and doves, and others sitting at tables exchanging money. So he made a whip out of cords, and drove all from the temple courts, both sheep and cattle; he scattered the coins of the money changers and overturned their tables" (John 2:14–15).

How many people had been into that temple and seen the same money changers? How many times had Jesus' disciples observed the compromise and corruption that was in the Father's house? Yet they had let their apathy adjust their worship to fit around the activities of the money changers. They had accommodated the trading of animals while they were trying to bring their offerings. But Jesus was not about to share this space with market sellers. He wouldn't cohabit with compromise, for He knew the temple was His zone and the corrupt money changers had no right to be there. His passion turned that environment around instantly as He began to turn over the tables. Some people may have thought His behavior was an overreaction, but Jesus was revealing how dangerous their indifference had become.

So what about us? When we walk into areas in our community, ministry, and relationships where attitudes, mind-sets, and behaviors have moved in that don't belong, do we have the same passion to turn things around? Are we willing to risk being misunderstood so we can make a stand? Where has our silence given ground to compromise? Where do you need to turn a few tables, show something the door, clean your house?

It was said of Jesus' behavior, "Zeal for your house will consume me" (John 2:17). Jesus wasn't a consumer of the house, just going for what He needed; He was consumed by it. He wasn't a visitor to that zone; He owned it. Jesus didn't just turn up; He had come to turn things around.

Now we must ask, is the same true of our lives? What is the motivation of our hearts? Are we consumers preoccupied with our list of desires and demands, or have we allowed a much bigger cause to overtake our hearts, causing us to become consumed for God's kingdom cause? Consumers will never change the world, but those who are consumed are a force to be reckoned with.

SEVEN

A PERMANENT INVESTMENT

AS WELL AS LEADING A CONGREGATION IN BRADFORD, England, my husband and I also have the privilege of pastoring a congregation in Belfast, Northern Ireland. This city is famously known for its longstanding troubles and tensions. I remember when I went to Northern Ireland for the first time and drove around the neighborhoods, seeing the walls of graffiti portraying religious allegiances and artwork of gunmen and the fights they were a part of. I recall seeing the barricaded police stations with barbed wire around the exterior walls and being told by our Northern Irish friends about the no-go zones in the city at night.

That trip had a deep impact on me; I felt fearful at times and deeply saddened at what was occurring in the name of religion. I left Belfast on that first trip convinced of two things. First, they needed a God intervention; and second, it wasn't something I was called to be a part of. When you already live in a struggling community, as I did in Bradford, the next choice for church planting certainly wouldn't be an even greater troubled city like Belfast. Yet God had something else in mind, and a few months later Steve and I sensed God calling us to be a part of a team that would start a church in Belfast and believe in the God who could turn all things around.

For the first few years in that city, our church family met in a rented hotel room, but over time we knew we needed to find a permanent space to be our church home. After some time God led us to an old warehouse tucked away in the city center. It was on a prime piece of land that was not even up for sale. As soon as we walked in this space, we knew it was perfectly situated to become our new church home. The more we committed to the process of acquiring this building, the more we saw God move obstacles out of our way until we eventually signed on the line.

On the day that we were to receive the keys for this building, we planned an evening with the church family to celebrate this next step and to pray over the warehouse where God had placed us. As my husband and I arrived in the city of Belfast for our opening weekend, after months if not years of relative calm in Northern Ireland, trouble broke out. Violence and fighting had erupted across the street from our new building, right in the city center, over a new political decision that divided the people of Northern Ireland. Our planned celebration was in jeopardy, as some feared that Belfast would regress into the problems of its past. We learned that the night before our arrival, petrol bombs were thrown and cars were torched in the city. As a result, police in riot gear were deployed, armed guards and police vehicles were posted strategically throughout the city, and the police had zoned off all the area around the city, where our new plot of land was, in order to protect it. If ever there was a picture of a city that needed a turnaround, it was here, and it was fully demonstrated on that night.

So we called a meeting with our team to decide whether it was safe to proceed with our planned event. We didn't want to endanger any of our congregation, but at the same time, we knew people would be disappointed if we postponed. After receiving input from various people and the police, we were advised to carry on with the event as planned, and thankfully we were able to proceed. The church families were contacted to let them know to be careful about their route into and out of the city, but that we would go forward.

Later that evening, after all that conflict, standing in the new facility with police stationed on all the streets around us, we watched with joy as our church family flooded through the doors. Some bundled up their children to keep them warm, others brought home-baked treats for people to enjoy, and young people brought friends. The faces of the people, full of excitement, hope, and love, were a welcome sight as they walked off streets that were chaotic and uncertain. Together we resolved to build a church that would turn their city around. We stood and passionately prayed that night as a church for the beautiful city of Belfast and committed long term as we put our seed in the ground. We were investing in what to many was a no-go zone. The dream of having a church in the center of Belfast as a place of hope, unity, peace, and healing had already been tested. God was looking for the first turn to be in our hearts as we committed to investing there.

DESOLATE DWELLINGS

In every community, desolation dwells. Within all our reach are the broken and isolated places where darkness looms, and we have to each decide whether we will be the ones to take God's light there. The very places we so often want to avoid, God wants us to go with His anointing, awakening the desolate to its destiny.

In Jeremiah 32 an incredible account unfolds of how Jeremiah became part of one of God's great turnarounds. Jeremiah was imprisoned by the king of Judah, Zedekiah, because his prophecies of judgment had upset the king. Jerusalem as a nation was under siege, and its people were in fear for their lives. *The Message* Bible titles this chapter "Killing and Disease Are on Our Doorstep." This is not exactly a great statement about a place where people may be living, but it was the exact address to which God was sending Jeremiah to dwell. Jeremiah knew more than most the ruin and devastation and sin and compromise that were upon this city. Because of the prophecies of judgment coming through Jeremiah's life, he had upset many people there, so now he was imprisoned in the place that God was judging.

I am sure Jeremiah on many occasions had planned his escape route. Why stay where you are not welcome, or as was the case for Jeremiah, where many hate you? Who wants to reside in a city that has been told killing and disease are on its doorstep? This was not an area anyone would want to invest in. As a prophet to the people, Jeremiah had carried out his professional obligation; he had delivered the word and could feel relieved of his responsibility. But God was not looking for Jeremiah to do a prophecy hit-and-run; He wanted him to commit to speaking and staying. God was looking for him to start a turnaround by doing something symbolic.

> God was not looking for Jeremiah to do a prophecy hit-and-run; He wanted him to commit to speaking and staying.

God's instruction to Jeremiah in a place of desolation was to invest. The way God asked Jeremiah to do this was by doing something unusual, as He instructed Jeremiah to buy a field.

Jeremiah said, "GOD's Message came to me like this: Prepare yourself! Hanamel, your uncle Shallum's son, is on his way to see you. He is going to say, 'Buy my field in Anathoth. You have the legal right to buy it.' And sure enough, just as GOD had said, my cousin Hanamel came to me while I was in jail and said, 'Buy my field in Anathoth in the territory of Benjamin, for you have the legal right to keep it in the family. Buy it. Take it over.' That did it. I knew it was GOD's Message." (Jeremiah 32:6–8 MSG)

The field Jeremiah was instructed to buy was on the outskirts of Jerusalem and was at that time occupied by an enemy army. Though this land was in Jeremiah's family line, it was now rendered useless and worthless to Jeremiah's uncle and was undesirable to any other tenant. Yet to God this land belonged to His people, and the enemy was living on borrowed time on their stolen field. God wanted Jeremiah's family to claim their inheritance, and in order to do that Jeremiah was going to have to have the faith to invest in a space his imprisonment wouldn't even allow him to go see. God wanted Jeremiah to be willing, from a place of containment, to start a turnaround process through his commitment.

The strength of our commitment will often demonstrate the conviction of our spirit. It is easier to say you will pray for the peace of a troubled place than to go and try to make peace, as we found out firsthand when we went into Belfast. God needed Jeremiah on this occasion to not just deliver but demonstrate His Word. God also seeks for His people today to be willing, when asked, to plant in the places others deem undesirable. He wants us to understand the power of permanence and refrain from the often ineffectiveness that a passing-through mentality can cause.

> The strength of our commitment will often demonstrate the conviction of our spirit.

When I was at university, I lived with a group of girlfriends for three years. We were temporary residents in a house together in the heart of the student village. Though we all chose to study in this part of England, none of us had any intention of staying there once our course was finished. Therefore everything about our actions and commitments was temporary. We lived in a rented house, we made casual friendships, and we didn't look for permanent jobs. Everything in our house spoke of a life of transit students, from the curtains attached with staple guns to the blue-tacked artwork on the walls. Our house contents could be packed up in moments and moved out.

Eventually I left university and got married. I remember being excited as we bought our first home. My thinking had now radically changed; I was committed to staying. I had chosen a place not just to do life but to build a life. I now had a permanent job, had started growing relationships, and was committed to a mortgage, a job contract, a church, and a marriage partner. With my permanent choices, my entire attitude and decision-making process changed.

Could it be that so often we don't see the turnarounds God has called us to make because we have become too comfortable and are going through life with a temporary mind-set when we should have a permanent one? Maybe we haven't turned around our space because in the back of our minds we are not sure that we are going to stay.

Permanence gives you an address. Your roots give you more rights; your willingness to stay creates an ability for you to have your say. We don't need to settle for complaining to the landlord about our environment when we can spiritually become the landowner and change it. God's answer to the derelict places is for His people to dwell there; His answer for the barren land is for His children to plant seeds and stay there.

God told His people who had been in captivity and despair to line up their lives with His Word and promises.

This is what the LORD of Heaven's Armies, the God of Israel, says to all the captives he has exiled to Babylon from Jerusalem: "Build homes, and plan to stay. Plant gardens, and eat the food they produce. Marry and have children. Then find spouses for them so that you may have many grandchildren. Multiply! Do not dwindle away! And work for the peace and prosperity of the city where I sent you into exile. Pray to the LORD for it, for its welfare will determine your welfare." (Jeremiah 29:4–7 NLT)

God is not looking for aimless travelers; He is looking for committed followers. We need to know what the issues are in our communities; we need to know where the hurt is so we can go help heal it. I have had to change my mind-set on different occasions and commit to being part of the answer in my own city and not allow myself to feel overwhelmed at times by its problems. I have needed to remind myself that I am called to be a solution and therefore my attitude has to come into agreement with God's turnaround power.

> God is not looking for aimless travelers;
> He is looking for committed followers.

A while ago I remember feeling challenged to step up my own involvement in the place where God had called my husband and me to be. Though we were living there, some of my thinking and conversation spoke more of my desire to be elsewhere. I began to understand I needed to stop adding to the negativity and instead start suggesting some positive solutions.

That shift in my thinking may not have been visible to those around me, but it soon became audible as the change in my thinking began to change my speaking. Where before I would criticize the place where I lived, I began to speak of the potential that God saw. With every new commitment to being part of the change I was praying to see, my actions also began to align. I wrote to local representatives and asked how I could better help serve in my local community. As a result of my conviction, I began to volunteer in my children's school and offered to address the children in their assemblies about the values and attitudes that could improve the school. In our neighborhood we joined local action groups and met with our neighbors to discuss how we could invest in and help the environment around us. The permanence in my heart began to change not just my confession but my commitments.

UNFAMILIAR PLACES

It wasn't long after my change of heart that I received an invite completely out of the blue to speak to a group of politicians at the Houses of Parliament in Westminster, London. These politicians were gathering on the opening of another term of Parliament to pray for our nation, and the subject they asked me to come and speak on was—you guessed it—"Turnaround God."

How the invite arrived in my world, and how they heard about the message that was in my heart, only God could have orchestrated. The incredible timing of this event again demonstrated to me that when I am willing to make a move, God responds by moving what I cannot. I remember thinking on the day I was asked to speak in this historic Chapel of St. Mary Undercroft, built in 1297, how incredible it was that almost a thousand years earlier King Edward took the initiative to build this incredible place for his servants, because they had asked him for their own permanent place to worship. The chapel had been built underground for the servants' use and was filled with ornate artwork and carvings. It is amazing to think how servants without power or title had gone to the highest power in the land to demand their own place to worship God, whom they knew held all power and authority. The historic list of those who have spoken from this chapel is remarkable, ranging from William

Wilberforce and John Wesley, to a suffragette woman who used that chapel to hide herself so she could secure her voting right. That same chapel, though hidden underground, became a place where God's people orchestrated great turnarounds on behalf of the nation. It was here that some of the most challenging issues facing humanity have been and still are being prayed about and addressed.

> **When I am willing to make a move, God responds by moving what I cannot.**

When I stood up to speak that day, feeling rather nervous and daunted, I began to share the essence of what I am now writing about: that God has a turnaround plan for our lives and communities and that it is our time in history to individually and corporately rise up. I wasn't invited to Parliament because I was the most gifted or influential speaker, but because I passionately cared and wanted to play a part in resolving some of the problems in my locality and nation. Having a desire and commitment to help be part of the answer is often all God requires from us. But if we disqualify ourselves by thinking certain credentials or qualifications are required before being able to take advantage of opportunities, we could miss the very thing God has in store for us. I would have never imagined that I would end up speaking in Parliament, but my passion that first emerged as a desire to help in my hometown became the very thing that brought about this opportunity to speak.

> **Having a desire and commitment to help be part of the answer is often all God requires from us.**

PLANTING ROOTS

Our best life is one that is planted, because our act of permanence in planting leads to the productivity and ability to
flourish. Psalm 92:13 says, "Planted in the house of the LORD,
they will flourish in the courts of our God." Just as a tree needs
roots to feed its branches, so our lives need to take root in God to
flourish. Any plant that is severed from its roots will eventually
die, just as the roses that are cut from the rose bush may bring
temporary beauty but eventually the water they are placed in
will be unable to keep them alive. We cannot treat the challenges
we are handling with a temporary mind-set. We cannot expect
the places we go to flourish unless we stay long enough to help
the people there find their place of planting in God. We have to
be willing to be planted in our commitment, in our choices, our
love, actions, and promises, if we want to see lasting change. We
can't opt for a vase-type relationship, making temporary turns
and superficial improvements, yet still expect lasting results.

> We cannot expect the places we go to flourish
> unless we stay long enough to help the people
> there find their place of planting in God.

When Jeremiah was told to commit to his family's field, he
took this instruction seriously by making a personal investment.
He didn't ask his uncle to give him the land for nothing or to
reduce its price because of its current tenants or its unlivable
state. The Bible records that Jeremiah paid the asking price for
the land and demonstrated his willingness to sow his own seed.
He demonstrated his trust in God's turnaround power by buying

a field that the enemy had already taken as his own. Knowing he had no way from his place of imprisonment to remove his unwanted tenants or to cultivate his land, he had to trust God to take care of the part he himself could not. God was not asking the impossible from Jeremiah but desired for him to accept the responsibility and do what was possible as his part of this turnaround. God then matched Jeremiah's obedience with His transformational power.

God is looking for us to have the same commitment in our own communities. He wants His people to come with a mind-set that is in it for the long haul, for us to make decisions that let God know we are not waiting for things to look better before we agree to play our part. God looked not at the problem but at you, His answer, and wants us to refrain from waiting for a success before we sow a seed. We must not allow the problems to become so exaggerated that we underestimate our own ability to bring solution. The harvest we desire requires the seed within our hands.

LOOK AGAIN

In the next few verses in Jeremiah 33, God begins to explain to Jeremiah how He will work where he cannot go and turn what no one thinks can be transformed. God instructed Jeremiah after buying his field to call on Him, to cry out to Him for the things that he couldn't figure out, to draw from Him the things that would turn this entire community around. God instructed Jeremiah not to look at this city the same way as all the others but to get a new perspective of the land others were forsaking and see how God could turn it into something beautiful:

But now take another look. I'm going to give this city a thorough renovation, working a true healing inside and out. I'm going to show them life whole, life brimming with blessings. I'll restore everything that was lost to Judah and Jerusalem. . . . I'll scrub them clean. . . . I'll forgive everything they've done wrong, forgive all their rebellions. And Jerusalem will be a center of joy and praise and glory for all the countries on earth. They'll get reports on all the good that I am doing for her. They'll be in awe of the blessings I am pouring on her. (Jeremiah 33:6–9 MSG)

Not only would God's restoration look different, but it would cause the people to sound different. He was going to renovate the exterior and rejuvenate the interior of people's lives. He was going to not just rebuild but also restore, and not just forgive the sin but add blessing to His people. Steve and I have prayed many times this same turnaround over the cities where we pastor. I think of the brokenness the war in Belfast has caused, the hurts that have changed the sound of people's lives from hopeful to hopeless, the addictions and abuse that have taken the innocent song from children in our streets and turned their laughter to fear. I am crying out to God to turn around not just what we see but what we hear. What about your community or your own life? Where is God saying look again?

God is asking many of us to look again and line up our behaving with our believing.

> God is asking many of us to look again and line up our behaving with our believing.

Jeremiah recorded that he had a witness verify his purchase of the land from his uncle, and as he had the transaction witnessed he declared over his investment the turnaround power he believed God would display in that land. Jeremiah was not only declaring what God would do, he was also aligning his actions with what he believed.

> So I bought the field at Anathoth from my cousin Hanamel. I paid him seventeen silver shekels. I followed all the proper procedures: In the presence of witnesses I wrote out the bill of sale, sealed it, and weighed out the money on the scales. . . . "Take these documents—both the sealed and the open deeds—and put them for safekeeping in a pottery jar. For God-of-the-Angel-Armies, the God of Israel, says, 'Life is going to return to normal. Homes and fields and vineyards are again going to be bought in this country.'" (Jeremiah 32:9–10, 13–15 MSG)

Do you have enough vision that you can see what God sees and act in accordance with where you are going, not what you are currently experiencing?

EVICT THE SQUATTER

The enemy has been squatting for too long in the places that God has given to us as our inheritance. He has become a permanent squatter in the places where we have had temporary attachment. In the relationships where we abdicate our place, the enemy moves in; in the areas of our lives where we don't take responsibility, he takes advantage.

It is time that throughout our lives and communities we take back the ground we have been given to invest. Imagine for a moment that you returned home one day to find that when you were out a squatter had moved in. After noticing an unlocked doorway, the opportunist took the chance to let himself in and help himself to your property, sleeping in your bed and eating your food. He quickly began to take over your home. When you returned and saw this intruder watching your TV and now wearing your clothes, I am sure you would immediately alert the police and begin the process of removing the squatter from your place. It would seem absurd to suggest that on your arrival home you decide you don't have the energy to fight this intruder, so you opt for trying to live with him instead! While this seems ridiculous in the natural, we allow this behavior to take place all too often in the spiritual.

The enemy seeks to squat in our homes, our relation-ships, and our communities. He is always on the lookout for an unguarded exit to enter through. Once he finds his way in, he stops at nothing to try to take over. Our level of commitment to protecting our spaces spiritually will determine how long we allow the squatters of poverty, darkness, fear, sickness, and sin to live in our land. We must refuse to accommodate the things we have permission to remove. We have to become forensic about finding every place that darkness is squatting and serving the enemy his eviction notice. When the people of God take their place, the enemy has to move out of the way. His darkness is no match for God's light. Maybe it is time for you to re-enter the places you have allowed the enemy to push you out of and remind him that you are here to stay and therefore he must go.

God is looking for people who are willing to change their

mind-sets and be committed to planting roots and flourishing in the desolate dwellings. It's time to look again at where we have been placed geographically, because the answer to the problems surrounding us is within God's ability to bring His transformational power through us.

Where has a temporary mind-set obstructed your long-term vision? Are you willing to commit even when the commitment may be costly? We are God's children and this is His world, so let's move God back into the neighborhoods and places where His people dwell.

EIGHT

UNLIKELY CANDIDATE

THE JOB DESCRIPTION WAS IMMENSE: IT INVOLVED TURNING the hearts and minds of the Gentiles toward God, building the early church while enduring terrible persecution and false allegations. At the same time, this job was to become one of the biggest contributors to the best-selling book of all time by writing just over half of the New Testament. This was no small calling; this job would require someone who could articulate and put into action God's Word with passion and persistence. God was going to handpick the person for this job, yet His choice would come as a shock to most. Rather than pick an established follower of the faith, God chose a murderer as his newest recruit (Acts 9:15).

Saul was the last person anyone expected God to pick to be the evangelist to the Gentiles. He was a known persecutor of

Christians and feared by those who followed the teachings of Christ. Saul had approved of the murder of Stephen and personally led many campaigns to torture and attack those who were committed to establishing the early church. Saul was one of the church's greatest enemies, yet God selected him to become the church's greatest representative.

God saw something in Saul that no one else could. Where most people could only see Saul's intimidating exterior, God saw his potential deep within. Even though Saul was a persecutor, from God's turnaround vantage point, he would become a preacher. Even though Saul was a maverick and murderer, God would turn him into an effective missionary. God was not assigning the Saul they knew; He was awakening the apostle Paul He knew.

God had seen within Saul the strength and ability for him to pioneer His church and advance the gospel. I believe that Saul's radical and determined qualities captured God's attention because He wanted to redeem and use them through the new identity He had designed for his life as the apostle Paul. However, there is often a delay between our prayers and their answers because of our inability to look from God's perspective to find the solution for the need.

When we face difficult situations, it is too easy to pray in a way that dictates to God how we feel that the turn should happen and whom He should use. God's choice and ours will not always match up. The early church certainly didn't expect that the answer to their prayers would be a murderer. That is why we have to stretch our ability to receive God's out-of-the-box answers. God sees every life from His turnaround perspective. His potential solutions are not restricted to the people who look the part or who have the necessary experience. God does not fill jobs the way you and I might.

| **God sees every life from His turnaround perspective.** |

OUT OF THE BOX

When God wanted to use Saul to reach the Gentile church, He also needed to find a willing servant to help search out this unlikely candidate. So He approached Ananias. As a committed servant of God, Ananias had prayed on many occasions for doors to be opened for the early church. Yet when God came to ask him to seek out the one He had chosen to open those doors, Ananias struggled with His request.

> Ananias protested, "Master, you can't be serious. Everybody's talking about this man and the terrible things he's been doing, his reign of terror against your people in Jerusalem! And now he's shown up here with papers from the Chief Priest that give him license to do the same to us." (Acts 9:13–14 MSG)

Though we may not want to admit it, we respond to God's call the same way Ananias did. Instead of being thrilled at God's out-of-the-box suggestion, Ananias was very disturbed at His choice. Rather than responding to God with great faith, Ananias questioned God's choice and even sanity at His suggestion, protesting, "You can't be serious." It seemed that this unlikely candidate was better left alone as far as Ananias was concerned. If I am honest, there have been times when I, like Ananias, have not been in total agreement with God's choice. I didn't want Him to use the person I didn't approve of or the one I felt didn't deserve advancement. There are times when God's selection will challenge your mind-set and values. Where you thought yourself to be inclusive, God's choice can reveal areas within us where we are excluders.

It is vital to learn how not to categorize people according to what we think they could achieve. We may see a place for the misfit like Saul at some point, but only after a lot of conditions are met—and even then, only for a select purpose and an even more select audience.

God's master plan for Saul was not to attempt to win him over with persuasive arguments. God knew that for this unlikely candidate to find his place, Saul needed to experience God's power and presence.

PRESENCE OVER PERSISTENCE

God interrupted Saul's journey with the power of His presence. Rather than using force or a fight to turn his life around, God let His presence transform Saul's heart on the road to Damascus. God revealed Himself to Saul, and in response Saul chose to follow God.

God was not going to force Saul into his future. Instead, He was going to introduce him to His Son.

All this time Saul was breathing down the necks of the Master's disciples, out for the kill. He went to the Chief Priest and got arrest warrants to take to the meeting places in

Damascus so that if he found anyone there belonging to the Way, whether men or women, he could arrest them and bring them to Jerusalem.

He set off. When he got to the outskirts of Damascus, he was suddenly dazed by a blinding flash of light. As he fell to the ground he heard a voice: "Saul, Saul, why are you out to get me?"

He said, "Who are you, Master?"

"I am Jesus, the One you're hunting down. I want you to get up and enter the city. In the city you'll be told what to do next." (Acts 9:1–6 MSG)

The crucial component in God's turnaround calling is God's presence. We must not confuse our job with God's. God may ask you to go to people, just as He asked Ananias to go to Saul; but notice that God did not ask Ananias to make Saul's turn. He didn't commission Ananias to persuade Saul; He simply asked him to go pray with Saul. When we confuse our role and God's, we can remove His presence and instead use our own persistence to try to push people into the places we think God has destined them to go.

> The crucial component in God's turnaround calling is God's presence. We must not confuse our job with God's.

We cannot force people to turn around through convincing arguments or even words from God. If we force people to change, it will become our job to be that person's enforcer of the change. Although Ananias would be used to help Saul connect with his future, he wasn't responsible for keeping Saul connected to God. Saul's encounter with God was what would hold him, way beyond where any amount of forcing could push him.

FINDING THE LOST KEYS

When I was a child, I had an old musical jewelry box. It was the kind that needed to be opened with a key and when it was unlocked, not only did you gain access to your hidden treasure, but a ballerina would also pop up and music would play as she twirled around. As the years went by, I used this music box less and less. It remained locked on the top shelf of my wardrobe for many years until one day when we were moving, I rediscovered it while packing my room. My once-precious box had slightly rusted and was covered with dust. After searching through endless drawers and containers, I finally found the key for my jewelry box. However, when I went to place the key in the lock, the accumulated rust made it impossible to turn. I remember in my frustration forcing open the lock, and as a result, the key snapped off in my hand, leaving the box tightly shut and the key broken inside. What could have been a discovery of a forgotten treasure instead became a huge disappointment as the damaged box and its contents were thrown away.

Even though the key and lock were designed to fit, they still needed help to turn. The neglect over time couldn't be fixed through my force; it needed something else. Had I taken the time to apply some oil to this lock and key, I could have avoided the damage altogether. A little oil would have helped the rusted lock.

God's presence works exactly the same in the lives around

us. If we commit to find the lost keys in God's kingdom, we also have to be diligent to cover any of the rust and damage caused by their neglect. We must resist the urge to force people into places we believe God wants them and instead let the presence of God work like oil in their hearts and lives, guiding them and leading them to where they were made to fit. God's power can liberate what our forcing will only frustrate.

> ## God's power can liberate what our forcing will only frustrate.

Often I have come across lives that seem to be sealed shut. These people have become victims of an impatient turner who forced more than they were ready for. God is far more patient with His people than we are with one another. His presence creates room for people to navigate their own change gracefully, rather than using forceful ultimatums that result in deadlock. God's presence opens hearts and lives, while forcing has the opposite result of closing and shutting people down. Ananias did not force Saul; he guided him through the kindness of healing prayer. God encountered Saul in a way that helped, not hindered, his turnaround. Saul's values turned, his heart turned, and his confession turned—and during those few days where he had been struck blind, he began to see differently.

When God calls us to roles and situations we feel ill equipped for, the last thing we need is for people around us to tell us what to do. We don't need any more confusion adding to our disorientation. We need people who carry God's presence and know how to apply it. When Ananias arrived, he helped bring clarity to Saul.

We need people who carry God's presence and know how to apply it.

So Ananias went and found the house, placed his hands on blind Saul, and said, "Brother Saul, the Master sent me, the same Jesus you saw on your way here. He sent me so you could see again and be filled with the Holy Spirit." No sooner were the words out of his mouth than something like scales fell from Saul's eyes—he could see again! He got to his feet, was baptized, and sat down with them to a hearty meal. (Acts 9:17–19 MSG)

LOST POTENTIAL

For several years I worked in the recruitment business, and every day, my role was to match potential candidates to the correct job. The interview sheets asked the same questions of every person. We would place each candidate in a certain skill category and salary bracket based on their answers to these questions. The process was so automated that there was no room for any creativity or those with unique abilities to shine. If a client had a certain job need, we would simply look in the right file and give him the corresponding candidate.

I will never forget the day I was left in the office to close up for the weekend, and as I was about to turn the answer machine on, the telephone rang. I picked up the phone to hear one of our major clients desperate to fill a job for the following morning. It was a standard position in their packaging department and we were expected to fill the post immediately. When I hung up the phone, I remember being annoyed that I hadn't hit the answer phone button sooner, as I knew all the people on our books had been assigned for the weekend. Desperately I rummaged through the filing cabinet and came across a folder with information about a young man I had not contacted before. I didn't even read through the employee's information sheet. Instead I phoned and asked him if he was willing to go. He was enthusiastic and assured me he would be there. So with the job filled, I left for the weekend.

The following week, I went to check on my client to see if the staff member I had sent had worked out. I will never forget the conversation that followed. The client began to tell me how the young man had presented them with a challenge. "Was he late? Did he not work hard?" I asked. "No," my client replied. "He was the best worker you have ever sent us. We just didn't realize you would send someone to a role like this with such disabilities." In my haste to fill the job, I had not read the part of this young man's information form that mentioned he was disabled and had been born with no arms. Now I realized why his form had been left in the cabinet. No one saw him as a match for any position, especially not one like the job I had sent him for. Yet in my oversight, a small miracle had happened. This young man had been given the opportunity to prove that not only could he do the job but he was the best we had ever sent for that role.

For years, all anyone had ever seen was this man's disability. He had been judged as incapable because of his physical limitations, when he was in fact more than able. He packaged twice as fast with his feet as the other employees could do with their hands. That young man became that company's next permanent employee. I have often thought back to that young man. His life was on hold in a form in a filing cabinet because no one could see what gift lay within him. God has so many candidates who are potential answers for our world, yet many of them do not look like the person you or I may have in mind.

Time and time again I have watched God raise up the most incredible leaders from the most unusual places. I have seen drug addicts everyone walked past turn around to become the business leaders everybody wants to be around. I have watched God take the most foul-mouthed bully and turn him into one of the biggest blessings. God has selected vessels to use that many would have discarded. He has revealed treasure in what many would have deemed trash.

God does not recruit; He creates. He can take any life and create greatness within it. God has not, and will never, put you in a filing cabinet, forgotten and deemed unsuitable. As God's people, we have to stretch our own understanding and enlarge our capacity for God's turnaround answers. We can't let fear of a Saul intimidate us and close our eyes to the answer that is the apostle Paul waiting within them. God needs us to look again around our lives for those we may have overlooked.

I   God does not recruit; He creates.   I

MIS-FIT

Have you ever tried to open a lock only to realize it will not turn because you are using the wrong key? Though the key may fit inside the lock, it will not turn and therefore the door remains tightly shut. The same can be true spiritually. Often we become frustrated that things are not turning around as we had desired, but we may need to stop complaining and start asking whether we have placed the right key in the lock. Are we expecting something to turn when the key we are using was not made for that lock? Are we looking at the wrong people to be an answer and overlooking the one God has designed as the answer?

In 1 Samuel 8:19, the people of Israel did just that. They rejected God's wisdom and decided that in order for the nation to be turned around, they needed a king—a king who was strong and powerful to represent them, like the other nations had representing them.

Israel did not want to search for a different key; they wanted their king to look like all the other kings. They didn't want to wait for God's answer; they felt they could fix this problem themselves. So they looked at what everybody else had and determined that was what they needed. Instead of waiting for God to reveal the right key, in their stubborn haste for a king, they settled instead for Saul.

It is too easy to fall into this same pattern of thinking today. It's like trying to use someone else's key in your front door lock and wondering why it won't work. We then struggle with disappointments and feelings of frustration when doors fail to open. If you have the wrong key, no matter how hard you force that lock, it will not open. Do not force what God is not endorsing.

❚ Do not force what God is not endorsing. ❚

Eventually, the Israelites' decision to make Saul their king went horribly wrong. God needed His prophet Samuel to move past his disappointment in Saul in order to go and find His appointed king, David. In 1 Samuel 16:1, God said to Samuel, "How long will you mourn for Saul, since I have rejected him as king over Israel? Fill your horn with oil and be on your way; I am sending you to Jesse of Bethlehem. I have chosen one of his sons to be king."

As the Master Locksmith, God knew the key that would turn the nation around would not be found in a palace; instead, it was hidden on a hillside where no one was looking for an answer. God had the right key for the lock, but He needed Samuel to be willing to go and find it. David was a lost key for the people of Israel, just as the apostle Paul was a lost key to the early church. Both of these men were God's chosen representatives, but they were not even on the selection sheet of God's people.

LOST KEYS

When our daughter was younger, one of her favorite pastimes was to take any set of keys she could find lying around the house and hide them in the most unusual places. I would spend countless hours searching high and low for the keys to our home, office, and car. The keys I had left casually on a counter became my most sought-after possession, as without them I was stranded in my present location. Without the right one, I couldn't even open the door to leave the house. Even though I had other keys that hadn't been taken by my daughter, I couldn't use them in the lock I was trying to open. I needed to find the right key for the right lock. I remember on several occasions searching everywhere, on top of cupboards and under beds, inside kitchen jars and in the washing machine. No one who was locked inside the house with me was able to rest until that lost key was found.

I believe God needs us to recapture that same passion for all the keys that have been lost. There are several parables where Jesus expressed the Father's heart for every lost person to be found. In Luke 15, Jesus taught the people about a woman who searched for a lost coin and the shepherd who, though he had ninety-nine healthy sheep, would not rest until he went and searched everywhere for the one that was still lost. We can't lose our passion for the search-and-rescue mission we are called to be a part of. We have to be increasingly committed to overturning every rock and searching in every ditch until every lost sheep is found. Once, you and I were lost, and someone took the time to search for us. Now it is our turn to search for others. Within each life that we unlock, we access undiscovered keys to open many more lives and situations.

> We can't lose our passion for the search-and-rescue mission we are called to be a part of.

There are keys hidden within the lives we walk past every day that may have within them the power to turn around the very situation in which we are currently stuck. Samuel was sent to search for the lost key that was David, and Ananias would be sent to search for the lost key that was the apostle Paul. Both of these men would have to look in places others had refused to go until they found the key that everyone would eventually desire.

When the prophet Samuel came to anoint one of Jesse's sons, he almost quit his search for the lost key too early, as he came across what looked like a familiar key in the form of David's brother Eliab. "Samuel saw Eliab and thought, 'Surely the LORD's anointed stands here before the LORD.' But the LORD said to Samuel, 'Do not consider his appearance or his height, for I have rejected him. The LORD does not look at the things people look at. People look at the outward appearance, but the LORD looks at the heart'" (1 Samuel 16:6–7).

To Samuel, Eliab looked like kingship material, but not to God. God asked Samuel to resist the pull of the familiar and keep searching. As Samuel stood in that room, Jesse's seven sons passed before him—and with every potential candidate, God made a rejection. What Samuel didn't realize was that with every no, God was guiding him to the perfect fit. In fact, that day God's answer was not even in the room; he had been left on a hillside tending the sheep. David was such a misfit to his family that they didn't even think him worthy of consideration. David was too young, too weak, and too inexperienced to those who knew him, but to the God who created him, he was tailor-made to fit the most significant position in the nation. David was the lost key that Samuel had been sent to find.

Our entrance into the world of those God sends us to should not be forceful but graceful. Ananias, though at first resistant to Saul's conversion, became a key player in Saul seeing where he was called to fit all along. God wants each key found and each lock turned. I have on many occasions used more force than faith; I have let impatience push when God's presence wants to bring to peace. I have used persuasion over prayer. Each time, the treasure that life's combination should have unlocked has remained firmly shut.

While not every situation we hope to see turned around has a blinding-light moment as Saul's did, or an anointing party as was the case for David, there will be a moment God creates at every turn He has destined to happen. Whether the change is in a person's calling, relationships, lifestyle, or destiny, every time when God positions, He sends His abiding presence. He eases the turns that most would say are impossible.

God is asking each of us to examine which keys are still lost. Where have we placed the wrong key in the wrong lock and become frustrated because things have failed to turn? Where have we overlooked God's answer? Where do we need to be willing to stop using the keys that impatient hands use and, instead, be willing to find the keys that only God's presence can access? Too many times when we fail to trust God, we create deadlocks in our lives. We shut down the very treasure God wants us to open and enjoy. I have come across situations where forcing has replaced faith. I have seen parents, desperate for their children's lives to turn around, force them to serve God. I have seen wives force husbands to attend church and ministers force followers to commit. All throughout their forcing, frustration has grown and the gap they were trying to close has widened, as the door in people's hearts they wanted to open has been sealed shut.

God's presence can loosen every lock. If God can turn Saul into Paul and a kid called David into a king, there is no one beyond His use or reach. The question for His people is, will we assist in the turns that we often don't even understand? Will we take God's presence to places we don't want to go and let our faith, not force, assist God's great turnarounds?

NINE

NOT QUALIFIED

NEVER ALLOW A LACK OF SUPPORT TO DEPLETE YOUR OWN enthusiasm. We cannot question our ability to succeed and then quit before we have even started. God's backing will ultimately silence everyone else's questioning. If we rely on mass approval for our every move, our progress will be painfully slow and the number of people we help will be reduced significantly. Even when we feel unqualified, terrified, or inadequate, God is still calling us to rise up and take the next step.

> Even when we feel unqualified, terrified, or inadequate, God is still calling us to rise up and take the next step.

Eight-year-old Josiah was used to his life in the palace. As the son of the king of Judah, servants took care of Josiah's every need, and he did not lack any material possession. Josiah was not only carefree but lived extremely comfortably. However, everything changed when his father, King Amon, was assassinated. King Amon's trusted advisers turned against him and arranged his murder, leaving Israel without a king to bring direction and order. The law said the kingship had to go to the next in line, so this duty was now about to become Josiah's responsibility. Josiah went to sleep that night as a kid, but he would awake the next day with the news that he was now the king. His advisers may have hoped this young boy would defer from his duties, and nobody expected that he would take on the mantle of king. Yet Josiah, at age eight, surprised an entire nation when he not only accepted the crown but embraced the responsibility entrusted to him to turn his nation around.

FROM KID TO KING

This kid rose to the challenge that his kingdom placed upon his very young shoulders. I am sure there were many at the coronation of Josiah who felt their kingdom was doomed as they now had an inexperienced child in charge. Josiah must have awkwardly accepted the crown his father had worn before him. As it sat on his head, several sizes too large and far too heavy for him to hold up unaided, Josiah and all the people observing would have been only too aware of how ridiculous this looked. Their new leader's feet couldn't even reach the floor when he sat on the huge throne. Added to his immaturity and lack of experience was the reality that the kingdom he was now given to govern was in a terrible state. There had been war after senseless war and the nation had become one of mixture and compromise, as many false gods had become the chosen idols of worship.

Josiah didn't receive a clear handover or training. He was not set up to succeed. In fact, the opposite was true. Josiah was surrounded by sin and lacked any support. His father had allowed for compromise and every evil practice to take place during his reign. There was widespread immorality, and many false gods were worshipped. Yet Josiah's legacy is recorded in 2 Kings 22: "Josiah was eight years old when he became king, and he reigned in Jerusalem thirty-one years. . . . He did what was right in the eyes of the LORD and followed completely the ways of his father David, not turning aside to the right or to the left" (vv. 1–2).

Amid all of the compromise, this young king did not deviate from the path God had entrusted him to take. He did not refuse his turn, nor did he abdicate it to someone else. Josiah remained focused and turned the story of his family's legacy around.

FOOTSTEPS TO FOLLOW

Though the crown did not fit, Josiah chose to wear it anyway. He accepted that his new title would mean accepting the responsibility before him to turn an entire nation around. Where most would have expected excuses and a neglect of duties, Josiah set about the work required to turn his people back to God. Therefore, it is worth examining what Josiah chose to spend the next years of his life doing as he strategically began to make this turn possible. This young king applied principles that not only changed his nation but became the basis for one of the greatest turnarounds a king had ever achieved.

Scripture says that Josiah chose to follow in the footsteps of King David. Josiah realized that the example of his own father would not help him know how to make the turn, so he looked for an example that would not only encourage him but spur him forward in the decisions he would have to make. Like Josiah, David was also a kid when he began the journey that led him to become king, and Josiah drew strength from the fact that someone else had gone before him and faced similar challenges. So often we allow our own inadequacies to cause us to question our abilities. We can feel overwhelmed by the problems and isolated by the tasks we have been given. As a king, Josiah had no trusted advisers, since his own father had been betrayed and killed by his advisers. Yet he drew strength from another legacy. We cannot allow our turn to be missed because we feel inadequate—we must seek out the lessons and the legacy that can teach us how to turn.

When Steve and I first married, we felt God call us into ministry. Encouraged by family and friends, we stepped out. Yet I remember as we were taking on more responsibilities several people started to question my role. While they could accept my husband being in ministry, they preferred me to be more of a silent partner. I remember feeling isolated by some just because I was a female and therefore deemed not qualified to make a contribution. Then one day my parents took my husband and me away to a conference, and there I saw a woman preaching confidently alongside her husband. This woman was soaring, and as I witnessed her fly in her calling, I realized that I, too, could take flight. Suddenly I had new footsteps to follow.

We have to choose to find different footsteps to follow. Like Josiah, who didn't look at his idolatrous father's example but found in David a mentor to help him find the strength to turn, you must seek out the footsteps of those who have taken the turn you seek to make. Seek those who have gone beyond what you currently think is possible. Josiah left a legacy far beyond what many people deemed possible, but though the period in history was different, the God he served was not. Josiah looked back to draw from David's courage, so we, too, must look all around our lives. We must seek out the stories of world changers and history turners so we can be motivated and not isolated, encouraged and not overwhelmed.

> **Seek those who have gone beyond what you currently think is possible.**

SEEK FIRST

Josiah's first turnaround action as king was to turn his nation's focus back onto the God whom so many had forsaken. Josiah knew that in order for the nation to improve, the people needed to be pointed in the same direction. Josiah sought God for the strength to make the turn and the wisdom for how to turn.

Second Chronicles 34:3 tells us, "In the eighth year of his reign, while he was still young, he began to seek the God of his father David." Josiah was now sixteen years old. When other teenagers were pursuing their own interests, Josiah chose to pursue God. As king he had been entrusted with a position of power, and at any time he had the right to command people to not only serve him but worship him as their ruler. Yet King Josiah chose to humble himself and bow his knee to the King of kings. At sixteen he set aside his selfish ambitions and instead served his nation by seeking God.

When we seek God, it changes what we see and say. Josiah did not speak like those who had gone before him. He did not use his position for his own gain. His speech was guided by what God revealed to him; the more Josiah sought after God, the more clarity he had in turning his nation around. Josiah could have let his youth and inexperience lead the way. After the failure of his father and the rebellion in his kingdom, he could have allowed his frustration and disappointment to guide his direction. But he determined to seek God, just as his father in the faith, David, had sought God. He desired God's peace and presence to go before him. Josiah's seeking God secured success for his people's future; likewise, our seeking God will bring the same. Our frustrations may cause us to make changes, but it is only our seeking of God that will steady our hearts enough to make the turnarounds that can save the nations. Josiah's leadership was not reactive or impulsive, as it could have been because of his age. I firmly believe age is neither an advantage nor a disadvantage in our callings. Our success is steered by our attitudes, not our ages. If we are seekers of God rather than our own pleasure, then we, like Josiah, will take on the most turbulent of times and turn it around.

Our success is steered by our attitudes, not our ages.

Young King Josiah was surrounded by opinions and advice from those who held positions in his palace, yet it was his seeking that enabled him to know which voices to listen to and where to place them. Seeking God helps silence the interference that often distracts and drowns out wise counsel in our lives. We have to develop the habit of seeking God as a daily discipline so that we can attune our lives to the right frequency to be alerted to God's voice more than our frustrations, feelings, or peers.

My husband first came to England on a one-year visa. Toward the end of that year, we had just started dating, so he reapplied for another term. However, he was denied a visa so we had to decide what to do. I remember being advised by some people that this was a sign from God that Steve should not be in the UK and should return home. Yet we knew as a couple that God had called us to pastor in a church in England, and my husband had a huge desire to reach the young people in the UK with the gospel.

Our circumstances and the advice of others were suggesting that we alter our plans. It was at this point that Steve and I decided that we needed to silence all the opinions and seek God's face. We wanted to be guided by God, not by our feelings or frustrations. My husband, in his seeking God, came to a peace that we were to continue in the direction we felt God had called us to take. God gave him a word that God's office was bigger than the British home office that was denying his visa.

After failed attempts at sorting out the visa in the UK, we were told the only option was for Steve to return to the United States and start his process of application all over again, which could take months, if not years. In a time when so many other voices were offering us directions, we sought God and went to the United States. Within hours of arriving at the home office in Chicago, where we had to restart our process, we saw firsthand that seeking God always strategically guides our steps. Within hours we saw God turn things around. We went from closed to open doors and from frustration to the favor of God as we were granted not just a year's visa but an indefinite, permanent leave to stay in the UK. Seeking God had stilled our hearts and guided our steps. We must always prioritize seeking in our turning. We need to know which direction we need to apply our strength.

URGED TO PURGE

Josiah's seeking caused him to begin purging and purifying his nation of all foreign idols and gods. Second Chronicles 34:3–7 says:

> In his twelfth year he began to purge Judah and Jerusalem of high places, Asherah poles and idols. Under his direction the altars of the Baals were torn down; he cut to pieces the incense altars that were above them, and smashed the Asherah poles and the idols. These he broke to pieces and scattered over the graves of those who had sacrificed to them. He burned the bones of the priests on their altars, and so he purged Judah and Jerusalem. In the towns of Manasseh, Ephraim and Simeon, as far as Naphtali, and in the ruins around them, he tore down the altars and the Asherah poles and crushed the idols to powder and cut to pieces all the incense altars throughout Israel.

Josiah knew that in order to turn his nation around, he had to remove compromise. For too long, God's people had given themselves to following and worshipping other gods. Their lack of faithfulness had caused them to lose their focus. Where God's

Word used to bring definition and clarity, their many compromises caused dilution and conflict. Josiah needed God's people to cleanse their lives and to purify their worship. So he commanded his people to destroy all the idols they had set up in place of God. He demanded changes that would accomplish a turn in direction; his seeking God caused him to speak boldly to his people. King Josiah began to take authority where the enemy had been exposing for too long the nation's apathy.

So many times we can see the changes and turnarounds we need to make, but the compromise we would have to confront can deter us from even beginning to try to bring change. Josiah knew as he began the purging of his nation that people would rebel, but he also knew that God would reward his obedience and work with him in the turn he was initiating. When you seek God, not only will He direct you in what He is calling you to do but He will also anoint you for the task. Though Josiah was young and inexperienced in leading a nation, God came alongside him to establish what he was endeavoring to do.

> **When you seek God, not only will He direct you in what He is calling you to do but He will also anoint you for the task.**

God called Josiah to start this turnaround by addressing the sin and perversion in His people. This was going to be a turning that would require a conviction and confidence in God. So often we want God to start the difficult turns for us; we want Him to break the ground before we try to turn things around. But God wants to strengthen you, not substitute you. The more we seek God, the more we will see of what God wants us to turn around.

And as we seek Him, we have to allow His greatness to fill our hearts and minds so that we can look at all we are called to take on without becoming overwhelmed at the task. Josiah had positioned himself so he was more aware of God than the people. As he confronted his nation, Josiah knew that God was with him and therefore he silenced any fears of who may be against him.

Josiah risked being unpopular to do what was right. He went against the face of false religion and idolatry. He chose to confront what others had chosen to ignore. Josiah was willing to purge and purify even if it meant doing it alone. There are times when our call to purify may mean confronting the sin others are concealing. It may mean questioning the compromise in our own lives or challenging the bad practices that others are accommodating. This may not always be popular with people, but it will always be pleasing to God.

TIMED TURNS

Josiah knew he had little support for the direction he had chosen, yet he trusted that what God asked him to do He would enable him to carry. Josiah's willingness to start the turn was met by God's faithfulness. God had aligned for Josiah a partnership that would both affirm and confirm all he set his hands to do. God knew Josiah would need support to stand firm as he burned down altars and removed foreign idols from his land. God divinely aligned for Josiah a fellow nation turner who would accompany Josiah's righteous actions with God's restorative Word. This help came in the form of a young man who was also called by God from a young age—the prophet Jeremiah.

Jeremiah's journey, like Josiah's, started when he was very young. Though Jeremiah's position was not to serve as king, his appointing was to serve the same kingdom. He was not given a physical crown to wear, but he had been appointed by God to be a voice to his generation. However, Jeremiah struggled with his own feelings of inadequacy before he accepted taking his turn. When God asked Jeremiah to speak up for Him, Jeremiah's reply was less than convincing. He told God, "I do not know how to speak; I am too young" (Jeremiah 1:6). God responded, "Do not be afraid of them, for I am with you" (v. 8).

God called Jeremiah to serve Him at the exact same time as He had called Josiah. While both these young men felt alone, God had their lives aligned. So often God will choose for us the right partnerships for the purpose He has called us. When we agree to step out, we also come into agreement with the alignments God wants to make. Josiah's standing and Jeremiah's speaking were turns that were set to God's timer.

TURN THE DIAL

When I want to use my washing machine, I turn its dial to the setting I deem most appropriate for the clothing I have placed in the machine. Once I have selected the cycle and pressed the start button, the machine kicks into action. My first turn of the dial causes many other processes to take place to achieve the desired end result. Once the machine turns on, the door locks me out so that I cannot interfere with the instructions that have been given. The machine goes from soaking to spinning and back again because of my decision.

Our initial action has the same effect. Once we commit to our part in God's turnaround mission, we lock in the coordinates for all the other parts that are needed to make this cycle successful. Josiah's first turn as king set the destination for his nation to turn back to God. On that cycle God had programmed the right people to find Josiah at the right places. Jeremiah's arrival brought momentum to the turn that Josiah had begun as his words affirmed what the cycle of turning would achieve.

We cannot expect every resource, relationship, and circumstance to line up before we commit. We must be willing to turn the dial in the direction God has asked us to go and trust Him for the help to come. For every Josiah, God has a Jeremiah; He wants to match up His words with those doing His work. Every time we feel the prompting to step out, we must be willing to respond, as so often our responses are part of a much bigger plan. Maybe your words are the affirmation in the cycle of another. Maybe your contribution will enable the turning to move from soak to spin. We must all be willing to play our part and let God prompt our contribution. Maybe somebody is waiting for the word you have been given, and until you bring it they cannot complete the turn they set out to make.

> We must be willing to turn the dial in the direction God has asked us to go and trust Him for the help to come.

I remember at one point in my journey being unsure whether the direction I had taken was the right one. I was faced with a decision whether to become involved in a new area to turn a ministry around. I knew this would be a huge commitment, demanding time, money, and energy. Yet I also knew that I needed to trust God to help me make the turn. It was not until I committed to the decision that things began to line up. I remember once I committed to the turn feeling so discouraged and wondering if this was the right call.

Later that morning a staff member brought me a note that had been hand-delivered to our offices. The note was a word of affirmation detailing things that I had just prayed about to God and that no one else could know were the concerns of my heart. When I asked where this note had come from, I was informed a gentleman left it and said God told him to write it. He said that as he went to post it he felt prompted by the Spirit that the note needed to get to me today, so he drove past the post office and made the delivery himself. That note not only encouraged me but moved me from soak to spin. It sped up my resolve to keep turning, and as a result a new level of activity began to happen in an area where before nothing was happening.

That day, that man brought words that lined up with God's timing. Ever since then, I have determined that the moment I feel prompted to text, write, tweet, or hand-deliver the words God has placed in my heart for another, I will act upon it straightaway. God has a perspective of that life that I may not have; therefore, His timing is perfect for their turning. Josiah went from feeling alone and probably intimidated by the people his turns were offending to feeling affirmed as Jeremiah's words came just in time to keep the turn going.

God has aligned spiritually His Josiahs and Jeremiahs, and our ability to find one another rests on our willingness to take our turn on time. We must shorten the delays our own hesitation can cause. Jeremiah 1:2 says of Jeremiah, "The word of the

LORD came to him in the thirteenth year of the reign of Josiah son of Amon king of Judah." Jeremiah's timing was directly related to Josiah's turning. God had put them in the same cycle to take their turn.

As you are reading this chapter now, God has been speaking to others about the turns you are committing to make. He has set up your life for some turnaround help that you can only discover once you start the turn. Be responsive today; look for the contribution you are supposed to make in God's great turnarounds. Who is waiting for your words to affirm their actions?

> Who is waiting for your words
> to affirm their actions?

HELPING HANDS

God often chooses friends better than we could ever choose for ourselves. Throughout Scripture God sent partners to those who were willing to take their turn. When no one would support David, God sent him Jonathan—a friend who became more to David than any brother ever had and did more for him than any king ever could.

Likewise, God gave Ruth to Naomi. When Orpah chose to turn back, Naomi expected to journey alone, but Ruth understood God's timing. Even though there seemed no future for a young widow like herself, she trusted God's turnaround power. As she took her turn, she found herself in the field of Boaz, who made her his wife—and they became part of the genealogy of Christ, who would turn everything around with His arrival.

Elijah thought he was at the end of his service, but God had another turnaround helper to anoint in the form of his successor, Elisha. Moses took his turn and found Joshua was ready to turn alongside him. And the list goes on. For every willing servant who agreed to turn things for God, there were partners God had already picked. Don't let your position, popularity, or preferences choose the people who are a part of your turn. King Josiah had many people who were attracted to his high profile. He had many who would have sought an invite to his palace parties. But the people you need are often not the people who apply. Jonathan was not the obvious choice for David, as he was the son of the king who hated him; and David was not in Jonathan's selection of most desired friends, as he was the man who most threatened Jonathan's position as heir to the throne.

> Don't let your position, popularity, or preferences choose the people who are a part of your turn.

Elisha was a servant plowing his parents' fields and was hardly the most sought-after successor for the powerful prophet. In fact, when Elijah was about to end his turn and go to heaven, many other prophets came to see his great handover. No one saw Elisha as the worthy successor. Instead, Elisha faced put-downs, but these only strengthened his resolve to carry on. God's candidates for spiritual partnerships don't apply for the positions all the others want. They don't need to be seen in all the places others seek to be, for their purpose is not to be the star of the turn, but to simply play a part in God's great turnarounds.

Jeremiah did not show up in the palace boasting in his ability to hear from God; rather, he came to Josiah humbled and uncomfortable in the calling to which he was still adjusting. Both these young men came to an awareness of what God wanted them to turn around; and as they saw the magnitude of the task and the privilege of the responsibility, they tore their clothes and fell on their knees crying out to God. If we are to be the kind of people who are willing to assist in turning around nations, we have to not only say what God wants to be said but also feel what He feels for the people. God's message in every generation rests on the messengers who will not only carry His words but also demonstrate His heart.

PURIFIED FOR PURPOSE

When Josiah was twenty-six, he began to purify the land. Purging and purifying may sound similar, but they produce different results—and both processes are necessary to ensure a nation's turnaround. Josiah's purging removed the false gods and destroyed the idols. It cleared the way of influences that kept the people from God. Now Josiah's purifying would help restore the values God's people had lost and give them something to turn to. As Josiah purified the land, he began to repair the things that had been lost. He wanted to renew the people's focus on God, so Josiah had the temple of the Lord repaired and restored. He then began to purify their worship by bringing those who were in charge of the worship back to the places where they belonged. He purified the places where they brought their offerings and restored the altars.

Second Chronicles 34:9–13 records that Josiah sought to turn around the house of God by bringing back the skilled craftsmen. Josiah understood that in order to make this turn-around in his nation, he needed not only to remove the things that had become a distraction but also to restore what had been forgotten. Before we can turn around our lives, we have to be willing to purge our hearts and minds of all the things that seek to distract us and then commit to build disciplines that keep us facing in the direction we want to turn. We can't rebuild until we have removed the things that hold us back. As Josiah committed to this process, verse 14 describes how their actions led to the rediscovery of the lost book of the Law that had been given through Moses. Josiah's purging led to the discovery of the Word and commandments of God.

In every turnaround commitment, there will be a recon-nection with the truth of God's Word. Josiah's uncovering of the book of the Law recentered God's Word among his people. God's truth became their guide as Josiah had the book opened and God's people aligned their lives to His truth. The Word of God cannot be removed from our turning process. It is in His Word that we find the confirmation we often need to keep moving forward. We must centralize the Word, and in so doing we will find it facilitates our turning.

Josiah turned his people back to God. He turned his nation from destruction to devotion. Every step he embraced in this process was necessary and holds within it a lesson for our own lives. We do not discover where to turn until we seek God, and it is our seeking that will demand from our lives a purging. God will highlight the things we need to remove, and then He will cause us to restore those things that have been lost. Josiah turned to God Himself before anyone else turned.

MAKE A VOW

King Josiah called the people to one more instruction as he requested that all his people make a pledge to God. He wanted their turning affirmed by their own commitment to love and serve God. Josiah had brought his nation so far on this turning journey, but he now wanted them to commit to keep the commitment they had made. This pledge brought closure to the destructive cycle that the nation of Judah had been on. They articulated a vow that reconnected their faith and their focus.

We also need to seal our commitments and be willing to pledge to the direction we have been destined to take. However difficult it may become, our vow to finish will prevent us from living on a repeat cycle. Josiah understood the power of his pledge when at age eight he agreed to become king, and he ensured that what he said he would do, he would see it through to completion no matter how hard the opposition.

As Josiah's final act of the turnaround he led, he made this pledge:

> Then the king called together all the elders of Judah and Jerusalem. He went up to the temple of the LORD with the people of Judah, the inhabitants of Jerusalem, the priests and the Levites—all the people from the least to the greatest. He read in their hearing all the words of the Book of the Covenant, which had been found in the temple of the LORD. The king stood by his pillar and renewed the covenant in the presence of the LORD—to follow the LORD and keep his commands, statutes and decrees with all his heart and all his soul, and to obey the words of the covenant written in this book.

Then he had everyone in Jerusalem and Benjamin pledge themselves to it; the people of Jerusalem did this in accordance with the covenant of God, the God of their ancestors. (2 Chronicles 34:29–32)

At age thirty-nine Josiah died, leaving behind him a legacy few other kings had achieved. Josiah turned around an entire nation back to God. This eight-year-old boy took his turn seriously. He aligned his life with God's power and rewrote history. Josiah's reign is a challenge for all of us—in just thirty-one years, Josiah turned the focus of an entire generation. Where he could have been excused from taking his turn as an inexperienced and underage king, he accepted the challenge set before him and God sent him the assistance he needed. Josiah knew the crown did not fit, yet he wore it anyway and soon found that he had grown into the responsibility he had chosen to accept.

God is looking for us to have the same confidence to accept the challenge even though it may seem daunting. We must trust that as God directs our turnings we will discover our true callings, and what once seemed ill-fitting our turnings will cause us to grow into. Josiah refused to be intimidated by the voices around him. His seeking turned up the volume on God's still, small voice within him. If we are to embrace our challenge, we must do the same.

> **We must trust that as God directs our turnings we will discover our true callings.**

Josiah's story paints a picture of what is possible and removes the excuses that we all too often hide behind. We need to re-examine our own time frame for God's turning. Maybe we have said, "It could never happen in my lifetime," but Josiah proved it clearly can. We cannot settle for turning around just our lives if God is calling us to lead a nation into their turn-around. God has many crowns for His children to wear, and as heirs of the King we have to be willing to take on kingdoms. So my advice is, even if the crown doesn't fit, wear it.

TEN

REMOVING RESTRICTIONS

FOR MANY YEARS OF MY LIFE AS A TEENAGER, I WAS EXTREMELY sick. I developed symptoms of constant vomiting and extreme weight loss that no doctor seemed to be able to diagnose. Countless doctors gave my concerned parents differing opinions, ranging from severe anorexia to being an attention seeker, yet none could find the source of my sickness. As the doctors debated, my condition worsened. Eventually my body began to shake and have frightening convulsive fits, as my organs seemed to want to shut down.

One evening, I recall leaving a doctor's office with my father, exhausted from yet another baffled doctor and a wrong diagnosis. I was sobbing in frustration. My dad assured me that we would not quit until we found the source of this sickness that had brought my energy and dreams to a grinding halt. I was desperate for a breakthrough, yet it seemed no one could discover the source of the problem. During this time I endured stomach examinations, endoscopies, blood tests, and X-rays. My arms resembled a pincushion from all the needles, and my body was exhausted from all the invasive tests.

Then one day, we went as we had on many occasions to our local doctor to try to alleviate my increasing sickness. But that day my father decided enough was enough. He announced we were not going to leave until someone found the source of this sickness. As we entered the doctor's office, he explained that we would be staying there all day until someone figured out what was wrong. By this time, my weight was dangerously low, I was severely dehydrated, and the quality and enjoyment of my life had gone.

That day there was a junior doctor covering our regular doctor's appointments, and in his surprise at our determination to stay, he went immediately to fetch all his freshly studied textbooks from the shelves. He sat reading, researching each symptom, and then said the words we had been waiting for: "I think I know what this could be!" He started explaining how there was an illness that, though rare, presented many of the same problems I was experiencing. Suddenly tears of relief flowed as I realized we might have found the starting point of our turnaround miracle.

The doctor quickly checked me into a hospital where I had become a frequent attendee; only this time, the tests ordered were very different. This doctor believed that the illness I had was within my pituitary gland, which would require a brain scan to verify, while in all my previous hospital visits the doctors had only looked at my abdomen and blood. This diagnosis identified the cause of my sickness, and after several tests the results came back with a clear result. They had found the source of the problem: a condition called *diabetes insipidus.* My body had been unable to hold water for many years, and as a result I had suffered from severe dehydration causing weight loss, sickness, fits, and fatigue. In that moment of diagnosis came such huge relief as I now knew the source of the real problem. I was even more relieved to receive the correct treatment to regulate the missing fluid in my body. For years I had suffered from the restrictions of a failing body, and now I was given the possibility of not only regaining my health but rediscovering my zest for life.

LOCATING THE SOURCE

My turnaround was not possible until we located the source of the problem. Though many other doctors had prescribed medication, they were only dealing with the symptoms while the source of the sickness remained unchecked. Therefore my fundamental health problems progressively worsened. So often our turnarounds can be jeopardized by our inability to locate the source of the real restrictions we are dealing with. Spiritually we have to find tenacity and commitment to go to the source of each situation we want to see turned, to treat the source and not just the symptom. Too many times we can accept the wrong diagnosis or can take a premature prescription to fix things, while the real underlying problems are allowed to fester. Our willingness to seek and find the source of the problems will affect the success of our turnarounds.

We sometimes avoid the source of our problems because we know that if we reveal our real feelings or insecurities, then we will become more vulnerable. We can work so hard at perfecting answers so that we don't let people see our internal turmoil. Yet if we are unwilling to go to the source, we will not see permanent changes. I have seen people's lives come to a grinding halt because they have been covering over root issues in their relationships, lifestyles, or businesses that were causing foundational damage. Though they had asked for prayer or sought counsel, they refused to be open and honest about the source.

> If we are unwilling to go to the source,
> we will not see permanent changes.

HONESTY HEALS

I remember sitting with one family who had hidden their son's addiction from everyone, excusing his frequent absences and lying about how they were doing as a family. They did not want anyone to know the nightmare in which they had found themselves. Then one day the addiction got so bad they cried for help, but by this time it had escalated into a life-and-death situation. Their embarrassment at the source of the dysfunction had caused them to remain silent, and their silence intensified the sickness.

The enemy wants you to conceal what he knows God can heal, and he often uses our own pride to deny our turnarounds. When I was ill, I remember being embarrassed about my situation and not wanting anyone else to know the details of my sickness. I wondered what people would think of me—would they believe the doctors who suggested I was anorexic or imagining the illness? I wanted to hide the fact I was so ill—after all, it looked as though I had no faith. Would people say I needed to believe more, pray more? All these irrational thoughts began to play with my mind and limit my ability to get the help and support I so desperately needed.

**The enemy wants you to conceal
what he knows God can heal.**

In 2 Kings 4 we find the story of a widow who needed God to help turn her life around. She had been married to a prophet of God and knew how God's Word was not only delivered but fulfilled. Yet when her husband passed away, she was faced with circumstances for which she was unprepared. This widow who had faithfully served God now went from married to bereaved; from feeling safe to being terrified for her future; from provided for to facing poverty so extreme that she could lose her two sons because of her crippling debts. I am sure this widow had tried to fix her own situation on many occasions. She would have tried to manage alone as she attempted to take care of the mounting debts so that her family did not go hungry. Yet, despite all her attempts to fix things, the problems remained. So in an act of frustration she cried out for help to turn things around.

CRYING OUT

The crying-out moment is something we all need to discover how to do. Often we are better at covering up than crying out, but our honesty is essential to the turnaround process. When the widow cried out to the prophet Elisha, she went to someone she knew would know how to help. Elisha had been a part of many of God's great turnarounds; he had seen miracles and knew that nothing was too far gone for God to turn.

Often in our places of failing or limitation we can avoid being around those who seem to be prospering or fulfilled. Their fullness can irritate our brokenness, yet we have to find a way to bridge this gap as we will never turn things around if the only people we turn to are the ones who are stuck in the same places of limitation. Though it may be more comfortable to share our concerns with those who seem to have even more problems than ourselves, it will not help us deal with our source issues. We have to be humble enough to cry out for help to those who have found a way out of the things that are holding us back. Why do we so often reinvent the wheel when we could be discovering new roads? We need the humility to learn from those who have navigated what is holding us back and ask for directions from those who are further down the road we want to travel on. The widow no doubt had cried with her sons and with her friends, but all that crying had not solved the problem. Therefore for her turnaround to start, she needed to identify to whom she needed to cry out.

As parents, spouses, leaders, teachers, employees, employers, and friends, there are many different hats we can all be called to wear. Limiting the places we cry out cannot lock us up. I have learned that the more I want to turn around, the more strong relationships I need to build. I need to find those who know how to turn their families around and those who know how to turn the good ideas into reality. I want to find those who have turned injustice around and those who are turning entire communities around. Our turnarounds will demand from us the willingness to seek out wisdom and cry out for the help of those who know how to take the turn we need to make.

FOLLOW HIS INSTRUCTIONS

As the widow cried out to the prophet of God, she waited for his reply. Aware of her lack and extreme need, the widow was looking now to Elisha for some relief. She reminded him of her husband's faithful service as a prophet and maybe in her mind felt that Elisha now needed to take care of this situation for her. Yet Elisha's answer was going to challenge this widow further as he had no instant miracle to give her; instead, he was going to ask her to play a critical part in the turnaround she needed. Elisha told her to go back in her house and open her empty cupboards, the same cupboards she had opened on countless occasions looking for food for her starving family and yet had found nothing. He was sending her back to the source of her lack to start the flow of her supply.

When we cry out, we need to be willing to follow the instructions we receive. The widow was crying out to a man of God who lived outside of her restricted thinking. When you live with limiting circumstances for a long time, it starts to shut down your ability to see any possible way forward. This widow who was starving and desperate was exhausted from her relentless debts, and her hunger and lack were restricting her perspective. Maybe, in response to her cry for help, she had expected God to provide immediately for her needs. Maybe she was expecting a cash advance to cover her debt, but she was not prepared for an answer that would send her back to her own cupboards. God's turnarounds will require our embracing of new thoughts. God's instructions in the midst of our limiting circumstances are so often not just about our answer but also about redefining our margins of where we have put God.

> When we cry out, we need to be willing to follow the instructions we receive.

I have never been very good with gadgets and am not a fan of reading the instruction manuals of any of the appliances I have ever bought. I would much rather rely on someone else's knowledge than try to decipher it for myself. Recently, I was with a friend who had the same phone as mine, but she was able to use it for many more things than I knew it was even capable of doing. She was montaging photos, editing videos, and shortcutting processes that would take me hours to complete! Both phones were exactly the same, only mine had limited ability—not because it was made that way, but because I had failed to maximize its capacity by refusing to read the instruction manual. I had used the phone for its most basic functions when it was able to offer me so much more. My lack of knowledge limited its potential.

The discovery that my phone had just as much capacity as my friend's caused me to go back and seek further instructions to find the potential that had been there all along. This is so often the difference between our lives and the lives of those around us. It is not that some people have been given more functions to facilitate their turnaround, but they have learned how to follow their instructions. God has the ultimate manual for your miracle, so you have to be willing to follow His lead even when it seems to make no sense.

> God has the ultimate manual for your miracle, so you have to be willing to follow His lead even when it seems to make no sense.

This widow followed Elisha's instructions and she went back inside her house to her empty cupboards. As she opened them, her eye caught a little jar of oil that she had been overlooking. So great was this widow's need that this tiny bit of oil seemed too pathetic to use. Her huge problems had caused her to minimize her potential and forget about the little that she had. Elisha was asking her to trust God, who had the instructions to turn this little into more than enough.

We need to accept the things we can so often argue about. Many of God's miracles have come from places and people most of us would never use or even consider as an option. I am sure Daniel didn't know God could seal shut a lion's mouth, but that was the way God chose to bring solution to his situation. I am sure the three young men would have preferred an intervention before they were thrown into the fiery furnace, but instead their answer was inside the fire—a place where most of us would only be able to see certain death. I am sure it confused God's people when they were told to circle the walls of the city of Jericho and then shout for the walls to fall down. That may have seemed a ludicrous instruction, but their willingness to obey secured their victory that day. There may be times when God's answers look as though they make no sense, but we have to learn that God's unlimited nature will lead us to some unusual answers.

God's unlimited nature will lead us to some unusual answers.

The widow must have felt embarrassed to bring out that little jar of oil, but if God says bring it, we need to obey. He knows what is within your cupboard better than you do and sees worth in the very thing you have deemed worthless. God's instruction challenged the widow to leave her house and collect from her neighbor's emptiness. The very people she had tried to conceal her problems from she now had to approach for help. Yet she wasn't going to go and ask them to provide her with something that would lessen her lack. She could have understood asking her neighbors to help take care of her needs by lending her some oil or supplies, but instead God was asking her to increase her lack by adding more empty vessels to her empty cupboards.

EMPTINESS

Emptiness is one of the most challenging things we have to deal with, and it can be one of the main reasons that things around us do not improve. When we run out of resources, we tend to restrict our believing. When we feel a lack of support, we decide to not try reaching out. When we feel empty of hope, we are tempted to quit. In my own journey, I have found that emptiness can often intimidate my own ability to believe God for a better future. I remember once arriving to teach at an event only to find a room full of empty seats. People who were expected to turn out did not come, and inside my heart I felt such disappointment. I began to feel disillusioned and questioned the value of my teaching that evening. I had a bad attitude, all because of some emptiness in the room.

At that precise moment, I remember God challenging me that I must turn my attitude around if I wanted to see the emptiness filled. I had to overcome the emptiness by letting it draw faith and passion out of my heart to see God's house full. That night something in my own heart changed as the emptiness that at first intimidated me now inspired me. My perspective had shifted and I began to pour my life out to God. That night, God did some amazing healings and salvations, but first God had to take me back to a source of intimidation that I did not even know I had. I had to deal with my doubts that emptiness had caused in different areas of my life.

Later I had to learn how to find a way to turn around when I was told that I was barren and had an empty womb. My husband and I found the faith to face a lot of empty chairs when we started new churches in difficult areas. We have had to face an empty bank balance, with more dreams than resources. Emptiness seeks to stop your turn and stare you down through intimidation. But we must refuse to back down and instead press on and allow His fullness to overflow.

Elisha did not want this widow's jar filled once; he knew that would not turn her life around. Instead God's plan was that He would flow through her to fill all the emptiness in the neighborhood. Once the widow collected the emptiness, she closed the doors of their home, shutting out all the other voices, and only then did she pick up the jar of oil and begin to pour. I can only imagine what her conversations with her boys must have been like as the oil kept flowing and the jars kept filling. Every vessel was full and their understanding of God's limitless ability was increased.

This incredible miracle began with her crying out to God, and it would end with her pouring out. The very life she had deemed empty now flowed with a miracle, and the very home that was a source of lack became a resource of great provision. Elisha did not fix this problem for the widow; he instructed her how to access her own turnaround.

GIVE IT A TRY

So often, like the widow, our own doubts cloud our contributions. Just as the widow thought Elisha would sort her problem, we can depend too heavily on others to be our answer. We need to be able to hear God for ourselves, as there are times in our journeys when the direction we take will look radically different than the direction others around us are taking. God wants us to rediscover the willingness to step out and try.

God asked the widow to start her own miracle. In that same way, He will often ask His people to start to change in the areas where they feel the least qualified. We must be willing to say, "I will give it a try." Even if your "try" seems like a small drop in the ocean of need, it will undoubtedly contribute to the turn you are asking God for. Let's consider some stories where God was able to turn situations around because someone was willing to try playing a part.

We must be willing to say, "I will give it a try."

In 1 Samuel 25:2–43, David and his men approached a neighboring rich landowner to ask for food and supplies. David sent word to the landowner, Nabal, because he had protected Nabal's land on many occasions from nearby thieves and troublemakers and therefore felt able to ask him to return the favor. Because of David's protection, Nabal's land had more than enough provisions for his own household and for David's hungry men. However, Nabal refused to be of any help and sent David's men away empty-handed. When David learned of this news, he summoned his men to put on their weapons and go teach Nabal a lesson for being so disrespectful and ungrateful.

David's men, hungry and now incensed, set out to inflict damage on Nabal's land and on its people. Somehow, one of the servants learned of their impending danger and in desperation sought the help of Nabal's wife, Abigail. Abigail was a gentle and unassuming woman—everything her stubborn husband was not. She was kindhearted, compassionate, and caring. Where her husband foolishly refused to show generosity, she was faced with her people's cry for help to stop this fast-approaching army before it was too late.

Abigail lived under the shadow of her husband's decisions, and up to this point she had not dared to disobey his instructions. However, on this occasion Abigail knew if she did not respond immediately, her people would be destroyed. Abigail was not a warrior or a skilled negotiator; she was a woman who loved God and now was faced with the challenge of how to respond. So she did the only thing she knew to do. She emptied her cupboards of provisions as quickly as she could and sent her servants to run on ahead as she loaded up the donkey and set out to meet the angry army already on its way. She did not waste a moment trying to convince Nabal to change his mind, as she realized that he was a wicked man to whom no one could talk. Abigail went into the dangerous situation armed with only grain, cakes, figs, and pastries. Her approach was hardly textbook in how to avert pending disaster, but it was wise. Taking food to a band of hungry men is always a winning approach. When she saw David and his army approaching, she threw herself at David's feet and begged for forgiveness. She took the sin of her husband on her shoulders and begged David to reconsider his intentions.

First Samuel 25 says that David was taken aback by Abigail's beauty and humility. Her willingness to try something in order to save her people moved his heart and he instructed his men to drop their weapons and turn around.

Abigail's seemingly foolish offering became the beginning of a turnaround not only for her but for her people. Nabal was drunk and totally oblivious to the whole situation. In the morning when he sobered up, Abigail told him what she had done. When Nabal heard this news, his heart failed him, and he died ten days later.

When David learned of Nabal's death, he asked Abigail to become his wife. What began with her commitment to avert danger turned out to be the beginning of her new future. Had Abigail stayed inside the containment of Nabal's opinions, she would have never unlocked the new things God had for her life. Her willingness to try caused a significant turnaround.

What began with her commitment to avert danger turned out to be the beginning of her new future.

AN INCREDIBLE JOURNEY

Many of us are familiar with the story of Moses and how he delivered an entire people and led those who had been in captivity for years into their longed-for liberation. Moses was a hero of the faith, the defender of the afflicted, the one who rescued an entire nation. Yet his life began not in the palace but in a place of danger. There was a conspiracy to end his life before it even began. The enemy tried to block the arrival of this baby whom he knew would turn his world upside down.

At the time of Moses' birth, an edict was declared across the land that every Hebrew baby boy born was to be murdered. However at that time, two midwives who feared God helped the Hebrew women find a way to keep their children alive. One such baby they delivered was Moses. On his arrival into the world, his mother knew his safety was in danger so under the threat of the law, She began to try to find a way to keep her child alive. She chose to do the only thing she knew how: to try. She made a homemade basket from willows and tar in which she planned to place her newborn baby inside.

It may have seemed absurd to imagine that a homemade basket would provide the start of the turnaround of her nation, but Moses' mom trusted God that if she would try to do what she could do, God would do what she could not. I can only imagine the fear and the doubts this mother had to silence in order to entrust her precious child to the unsafe waters. She released him onto the water in a desperate attempt to save his life, and God got involved. The older sister of Moses spied from a nearby embankment and saw that the basket was divinely guided to drift directly to Pharaoh's daughter, who then drew the baby out of the water.

This mother's willingness to let her child go had caused him to go from a place of danger into the very courts of Pharaoh and the arms of Pharaoh's daughter. Now Moses' sister decided to play a part in making this turn. As Pharaoh's daughter held the baby, Miriam spoke up and suggested that the princess could find a Hebrew woman to nurse the baby for her. This idea thrilled the princess, and she agreed to pay another woman to nourish the baby she now adopted as her own. In that moment, the very courts that had ordered baby boys to be murdered were now instructed to pay for this child's milk.

Moses' future was now safe; all because a few women tried to do something. If they had let the fear of Pharaoh's edict take this child's life, or if they had hidden him away for his entire childhood, then this nation changer would have never been able to fulfill his calling. We have to make the connection that all of our contributions matter. What if the midwives had not risked their own safety and the mother had not made the basket? What if the older sister who approached Pharaoh's daughter did not try? Their trying was the starting point of God's intervention to turn around the nation.

AGAINST THE ODDS

Let's look at one more example. In 1 Samuel 14, Jonathan and his armor-bearer were surrounded by the Philistine army. Jonathan, aware of the danger these men could inflict on himself and his armor-bearer, decided to try to take the ground he knew was rightfully his. Even though they had no specific word from God that he would have success or any army to back them, Jonathan said to his armor-bearer, "Come, let's go over to the outpost of those uncircumcised men. *Perhaps* the LORD will act in our behalf" (v. 6; emphasis added). In other words, "I am going to go try and take this land and *perhaps* God will give us victory." Jonathan had the courage to try and trust God to help him, as he was bold enough to advance and attack.

How many times have we failed to turn things around because we want more than a "perhaps" plan? We would rather let the enemy keep the land than try to advance in case we are outnumbered. But something about Jonathan's boldness that day drew from heaven a turnaround response. As Jonathan approached, the odds were stacked against him as he faced more than twenty strong men ready to fight. Yet God backed up Jonathan's faith, and he and his armor-bearer killed all the men who came against them that day.

A man and his friend's willingness to try defeated impossible odds. We must recapture this spirit if we want to turn our world around. Many of the odds we take on will require us to have little more than a "perhaps" to go by. We will have to face what seems impossible with our best attempts to try.

> A man and his friend's willingness to try defeated impossible odds.

Scripture tells us that God's thoughts and ways are much higher than ours (Isaiah 55:9), so why should we live in a way that has limited responses to the needs around us? We could bring resolve in places others have said are hopeless, but the answer will not lie in the places many have looked. We have to be willing to try, as these heroes in the faith who have gone before us have demonstrated. We can't be overwhelmed by the strength of our problems or allow the vast lack to close our lives down. On many occasions I have felt unqualified, yet I have felt compelled to try something. When I was severely ill, I was so desperate that I tried every prescription the doctors gave me. I just wanted to recover my health. In God we have to have the same desperation for the change He is asking us to make. We must be so desperate to see that change that we will push past our own embarrassment and discomfort and just do something.

> How many more miracles would we see if we would all have the courage to try?

Sometimes we only find out what we can really do by trying what we think we will never be able to do. So often I am reminded of this truth as I raise my children. Their willingness to try things is often limited by my willingness to encourage them to try. Unless I encourage them to try a new food, travel to a new place, or attempt a new activity, they will default to the levels I have lived within. Yet we need every generation to challenge one another to try. We need to be willing to spur one another on with our new ideas, which could be the start of our breakthrough. I want to build a life that tries to climb higher than what others believe is safe. I want to build a life that reaches people whom others say will never respond. I want to try to break the habits others are contained by. How many more miracles would we see if we would all have the courage to try?

Trying to fill all our neighbors' emptiness with our little oil sounds ridiculous, but so does trying to avert a war with cakes or placing your baby in the river or going into battle, two against twenty. All these would seem insane and doomed to failure. Yet though all these ideas seem implausible, they all attracted the turnaround power of heaven. God wants His children to understand that our trying opens the way for His turning.

ELEVEN

PERSONAL INVOLVEMENT

IF YOU HAVE EVER SPENT ANY LENGTH OF TIME AT THE GYM, you will begin to observe there are generally two types of members: the ones who have joined to get fit and the ones who are thinking about it. At my local gym it often amazes me how one will spend a solid hour working out, doing intensive cardio and weights, and others will head straight for the hot tub for a relaxing soak followed by cake and coffee in the café. When my family and I joined our local gym, we found ourselves falling into this latter category. My husband and I met with a personal trainer and filled out all the forms, yet when it came to the workout regimen we were given, it became more of a helpful suggestion than a serious commitment. While I went regularly to the gym, I was too intimidated to go in the workout room, as everyone seemed so much fitter and more knowledgeable than I was. Needless to say, after a while we realized that though we kept attending the gym we were not getting any fitter. Though we were paid members, we were not users of the equipment. The same can so easily happen to us spiritually; we can be on the membership roll of God's gym but not actually working out.

We need to ensure we don't develop a lifestyle that, because of our proximity to other people's activity, we mistakenly think is active. Our turning up does not necessarily mean we are turning anything around. We need to honestly examine our own lives to see how much time we are attending to situations compared to how much we are committed to involving. In my home church, we have a vast amount of outreach work that helps thousands of people every year change their lives for the better, but if we are not careful a pattern can develop between the outreach workers and the attendees. We can start to believe that because we belong to a place that is reaching people we don't actually have to reach anyone ourselves. We can create categories of people whom we believe are "more qualified" to reach people, and so we defer to them to bring the change that we pray we will see in our communities. We label people as the professionals, the evangelistically gifted ministers God clearly wants to use, and we disqualify ourselves and our own involvement based on a comparison of gifts or even a difference in passion. Yet God has called us all to bring change. We are all called to be salt and light agents who turn our environment around (Matthew 5:13–16). We can't rely on the few to reach the many—if we are going to see our world turn to God, then we need more people to move from attending to involving.

Jesus commented on this problem when He was ministering with His disciples. As they were among the crowds, Jesus said to the disciples, "The harvest is plentiful but the workers are few. Ask the Lord of the harvest, therefore, to send out workers into his harvest field" (Matthew 9:37–38).

When we look at God's people today, we have to keep monitoring how much of this harvest-to-helper ratio is improving. Every person Christ has reached must become a person who reaches out. Too often we are overwhelmed by the work that is to be done and spend too much time wondering where those who said they would help bring in the harvest have gone. We have to be careful we don't build in a way that allows some to sit back while the involvers are worn out. Do we have more people in the viewing gallery in God's kingdom than we do workers in the harvest field? Multitudes turned up daily to receive from Jesus, but multitudes didn't stay to help bring the harvest home. Even though many had been helped, they didn't turn into the helpers—and as a result, Jesus was left asking God for more workers.

> Every person Christ has reached must become a person who reaches out.

I believe God wants to awaken in all of us our privilege and responsibility to turn lives around. Many of us have become so busy doing life that we have forgotten that our primary calling is to be givers of life. We receive this incredible gift of salvation but then make no time to share it with others. We know a truth that can set lives free, but we are too busy to tell others about it. We have to examine our lives and ask ourselves, when was the last time we had the joy of leading someone to Christ, or laying hands on the sick and seeing them recover? Or when did we last still someone's storm or fight for their kingdom cause?

> God wants to awaken in all of us our privilege and responsibility to turn lives around.

MOVE THAT MUSCLE

Recently I did some research on how the muscles in the human body work. I found some interesting facts that have helped me as a leader address the worker ratio counts we can struggle with. The human body, I discovered, operates on two sets of muscles. The first set is made up of the involuntary muscles; they are small in number but crucial in function. The second set of muscles is made up of the voluntary muscles; they make up the mass of muscle in your body. The involuntary muscles have been given this name because they are primarily positioned around your vital organs, keeping your heart beating and your vital organs functioning. They are involuntary as you and I have no control over their function. If I told you to stop your heart beating now, I presume you'd still be reading—as you have no power to control the muscle that is keeping your heart beating. However, the voluntary muscles are the ones you do have control over. If I asked you to bend your right arm, you could volunteer that movement as your muscles respond to your instruction.

The Bible clearly draws a parallel between how the body works naturally and how it should work spiritually. So it is worth considering how this picture applies to the spiritual muscle of

God's people. The involuntary muscle of our faith could be likened to God. Without Him our hearts do not beat, and there is no breath in our lungs. God is all-powerful and almighty, and His power is involuntary in that you and I have no control over Him. He can forgive, restore, and heal without our permission. But the mass muscle of His body is you and me; we are the voluntary muscle, the ones who decide whether or not we will forgive, serve, stretch, and turn. Our effectiveness is based on our willingness as the voluntary muscle to become involved. If we only have a few muscles that are volunteering, we will have a huge handicap in our capacity and ability to turn.

The voluntary muscle is responsible in the human body for three things: agility, strength, and speed. And I believe the same is true spiritually of us as the voluntary muscle of Christ's body: our commitment and dedication will determine how much of the harvest we bring home. If we have unwilling muscle mass in the family of God, people who don't play their parts, then the speed, agility, and strength with which we could achieve the turnarounds God has asked us to bring will be affected.

When we neglect our parts, we add pressure to the few muscles that are overstretched, and often this leads to them burning out. We cannot reach our world with a depleted workforce, where only a few willing muscles volunteer. Our neighborhoods can't be reached only by an outreach core. The work requires all the muscle to volunteer to be efficient.

I am an avid runner. I love to run, but I spend most of my running hours on a treadmill. I think I am pretty fit until I go running outside and encounter the dreaded hills. It is at this point I realize I have muscles I have never asked anything of before. The flat terrain has only asked one set of muscles to volunteer their strength, but the hill awakens a brand-new muscle that was quite happy to stay asleep.

When we commit to be a part of God's turnaround calling, He will ask us to exercise every muscle, the visible and the hidden. Therefore, when we examine the worker-to-harvest ratio, we have to ask which muscle needs to wake up. We need to take on all terrains so that every muscle responds. We have to distribute the weight so every muscle sees its responsibility to involve. Maybe you haven't realized just how strong or capable you are to take on a turnaround, but once you volunteer your muscle to help bring in the harvest, you will find muscles you never even knew existed.

> When we commit to be a part of God's turnaround calling, He will ask us to exercise every muscle, the visible and the hidden.

INVITE OR INVOLVE

One of the reasons we often don't volunteer our muscles is that we are scared of the cost, the time, and the commitment that may be demanded of our lives. We try to measure our commitment against our already overstretched calendars, and we slot serving God where it is most convenient. But we have to be willing to increase our involvement. We can't just accept Christ's invitation for new life without then becoming involved in His calling to be bringers of that life.

Jesus volunteered His life so that He could get involved with ours. No company or organization can thrive by invitation alone; you may invite new customers, but if you refuse to become involved with them when they show interest, they will soon go back out the door they just entered. The same is true in the things of God: we cannot build the strength of our witness on just inviting people to attend a service or taking a flier for an outreach event. If we want to see lives truly turned around, we have to attach the invitation to its partner called involvement.

Our invitations let people know they are welcome, but our involvement sets the table for their arrival. An invitation tells the lonely they can come in, but our involvement offers to pick them up and bring them to a place they can belong. An invitation puts the expectation on the recipient, but our involvement transfers that responsibility to the inviter. This is why an inviting culture is much more effective than an involvement culture. The word *involvement* has emotional and personal associations. One definition of the word likens involvement to entanglement. Behold I show you why we don't volunteer to get involved!

> Our invitations let people know they are welcome, but our involvement sets the table for their arrival.

Yet Christ modeled a willingness to involve where others wouldn't even invite. He chose to get entangled in people's lives so He could then unravel them. Jesus often ate dinner with sinners and talked to those whom others would pass by. Jesus demonstrated a love that wasn't afraid to become involved. Religious leaders criticized His involvement. They were unwilling to volunteer their muscle to help certain people in certain places. They didn't want Him healing on the Sabbath or frequenting the houses of those they deemed unworthy. They had let their religion create restrictions, but Jesus came to remove them all.

GET IN SOMEONE'S BOAT!

In Luke 5 we see Jesus calling the first disciples. This was a moment that would change history forever as He was going to turn fishermen into fishers of men. Even the way Jesus called the disciples modeled His commitment to get involved. Jesus didn't invite the fishermen to attend a meeting; He went to where they were doing life and climbed in their boats. Seeing they had caught nothing all night, He even got involved in fishing and gave them the greatest catch of their lives:

> When he had finished speaking, he said to Simon, "Put out into deep water, and let down the nets for a catch."
>
> Simon answered, "Master, we have worked hard all night and haven't caught anything. But because you say so, I will let down the nets."
>
> When they had done so, they caught such a large number of fish that their nets began to break. . . .
>
> Then Jesus said to Simon, "Don't be afraid; from now on you will fish for people." So they pulled their boats up on shore, left everything and followed him. (vv. 4–6, 10–11).

Jesus' introduction to the disciples' world was by His involvement in it. He was modeling the ministry that He was about to call them into. Jesus caught fish with the disciples, and now they would go catch fish of a different kind with Him. How many times do we fail to model this example? We need a willingness to get into people's boats, to help in their immediate needs before we ask them to leave everything they know and follow God.

I used to invite a group of mums from the school playground to events we were hosting at our church. I would take a handbag full of fliers to the school playground, and as I was dashing off, I would say, "Please come." It never occurred to me that my fly-by inviting was missing its traveling companion of involvement. One day one of the mums commented how it was so hard to catch up with me, as I always seemed so busy.

I felt challenged by her honesty that though I was inviting, I was unwilling to involve. I was asking them to make room for my events when they didn't want to attend an event; they wanted me to stop so they could make a friend. So I began to accept their invitations for coffee that I had put off on so many occasions and left my fliers at home. A few weeks later in the church foyer I saw one of the mums from the school. She had decided to come that day without any flier invitation. She was willing to come to God's house because I had been willing to stop and have coffee at her house. Involvement had opened a lock that my invitation couldn't.

> Involvement had opened a lock
> that my invitation couldn't.

THE GREAT INVOLVEMENT

Jesus' ministry was all about involvement; from children to madmen, weddings to funerals, Jesus was there. In three public years of ministry with all of the responsibility He carried, He made time to become involved, and that is why in those few years He turned the world around. The disciples were not invited to join Jesus' Bible study group; they weren't isolated from people so they could receive His undivided attention. They were taken from the calm lake, where they would sit for hours fishing, to the chaotic seas of hurting humanity. The disciples, who were more used to spending time with fish than humans, left all they knew for an induction into their new calling.

Matthew 4:23–24 describes the disciples' new calling:

> Jesus went throughout Galilee, teaching in their synagogues, proclaiming the good news of the kingdom, and healing every disease and sickness among the people. News about him spread all over Syria, and people brought to him all who were ill with various diseases, those suffering severe pain, the demon-possessed, those having seizures, and the paralyzed; and he healed them.

This was nothing like the lake they had left. Madmen, cripples, and crowds were all pushing and pressing against Jesus' new interns. The disciples learned in the first few days of being with Jesus that this ministry was one that got involved. Whether the disciples felt qualified or not, Jesus was letting them see their days of isolation on the boat were over. We have to examine our lives and check our willingness to leave our boats. Even if the sight of the chaos has you retreating for the calm and familiar tranquility, as I am sure was the case for some of the disciples, Jesus knows that your destiny will be discovered only when He throws you in the deep.

When it was almost time for Jesus to leave the disciples, He called them together to remind them of what they were called to do. The title of this address is the Great Commission, and this is still the job description for all of Christ's disciples today:

> The eleven disciples went to Galilee, to the mountain where Jesus had told them to go. When they saw him, they worshiped him; but some doubted. Then Jesus came to them and said, "All authority in heaven and on earth has been given to me. Therefore go and make disciples of all nations, baptizing them in the name of the Father and of the Son and of the Holy Spirit, and teaching them to obey everything I have commanded you. And surely I am with you always, to the very end of the age." (Matthew 28:16–20)

This Great Commission was a call to a great involvement. Jesus was letting His disciples know, "I have given you authority to turn things around and the only way that will happen is if you go, make, teach, and baptize." These instructions were all activities that required their cooperation. Jesus did not call His disciples to retreat from the world but to go and turn it around. And He promised that as they did, He would provide divine assistance.

In Mark 16:17–18, Jesus said, "These signs will accompany those who believe: In my name they will drive out demons; they will speak in new tongues; they will pick up snakes with their hands; and when they drink deadly poison, it will not hurt them at all; they will place their hands on sick people, and they will get well."

Jesus made a connection between the miraculous and

involvement, a connection we must rediscover today. God's miraculous power is not elusive, but it is responsive. His miracles follow our involvement. We often want a supply of provisions before we will find a demand for them; but heaven's economy asks us to go to where the demand is so we can be a conduit of His power. The miraculous is not mysterious; it is simply attached to purpose. Christ said signs would follow the disciples' active involvement, and I believe there are many more miracles for us to witness as we help turn things around.

> God's miraculous power is not elusive, but it is responsive. His miracles follow our involvement.

IGNORE OR INVOLVE

Acts 16 is a well-known story to many. It's a picture of the miraculous power of God to turn things around. God sent a localized earthquake to shake a prison cell where Paul and Silas were bound. We may read this story as God's response to their decision to sing while in chains, but this miracle was in response to something that happened much earlier that day. God intervened because Paul and Silas got involved. Let's look at what preceded the prison miracle:

> Once when we were going to the place of prayer, we were met by a female slave who had a spirit by which she predicted the future. She earned a great deal of money for her owners by fortune-telling. She followed Paul and the rest of

us, shouting, "These men are servants of the Most High God, who are telling you the way to be saved." She kept this up for many days. Finally Paul became so annoyed that he turned around and said to the spirit, "In the name of Jesus Christ I command you to come out of her!" At that moment the spirit left her. (vv. 16–18)

I find this passage incredible and also encouraging as clearly the apostle Paul had some issues when it came to involvement. A young girl was enslaved and tormented and desperate for someone to turn her situation around, yet this passage lets us know that Paul at first chose to ignore her rather than deliver her. For three days she followed Paul, shouting and screaming until finally he became involved. God's apostle, who knew the answer to her torment, refused to stop for three days. Maybe Paul was aware that interfering with this slave girl would bring trouble from those who owned her. Maybe Paul was preoccupied with where he was supposed to be. He was on his way to pray, yet this girl got in the way—and now Paul had to choose whether to ignore or become involved.

It is also worth noting that only a few days earlier Paul had been stopped by another woman asking questions about his faith (vv. 13–15). Her name was Lydia, and she persisted also for Paul to give her and her family some assistance. On this occasion Paul did stop and even went to her home for dinner. Lydia, however, was a successful businesswoman, wealthy and able to provide food and rest to Paul and his weary team. The truth is that sometimes some people are easier to become involved with than others. To stop for Lydia meant there were benefits attached, but the slave girl seemed to offer only trouble in return for any help she would receive. We must be careful that we don't become selective involvers choosing to help those who can also help us, choosing to give where we can see an immediate return. We have to make room for both Lydias and slave girls. There was no one Christ would not involve with, and the same must be true for God's people.

Daily we have to make the decision: Do we stop for others or keep moving? Do we divert from our destination to help or just keep going? Many of the lives we are called to help turn around will not arrive at the most convenient time. They won't come problem-free or tidy. Yet God has them cross our paths daily as we are called to be His answer to their torment. We need a willingness to start the transformation of a turnaround encounter. We must push past all the reasons that we don't want to stop to find the heartbeat of our Father who wants to get involved.

Paul knew the moment He turned to the slave girl that there was going to be a costly involvement, which may have been why it took him three days to turn around.

> When her owners realized that their hope of making money was gone, they seized Paul and Silas and dragged them into the marketplace to face the authorities. They brought them before the magistrates and said, "These men are Jews, and are throwing our city into an uproar by advocating customs unlawful for us Romans to accept or practice."
>
> The crowd joined in the attack against Paul and Silas, and the magistrates ordered them to be stripped and beaten with rods. After they had been severely flogged, they were thrown into prison. (vv. 19–23)

TAKING ON TROUBLE

When Paul turned and delivered this girl, what happened next was exactly what he had wanted to avoid—she was now free, and Paul became bound. His involvement in her life led to his own persecution. If Paul had ignored this girl, he would not have ended up in prison; but if he hadn't ended up in prison, he wouldn't have needed that miracle jailhouse rock. The miracle of Paul's freedom happened because he had first fought for someone else's liberty.

If we want to see an increase in miracles, signs, and wonders, we have to give our lives to turning others' lives around. God did not call us to a great invitation or a great suggestion; He calls us to a great involvement that realizes His greatest interventions. How many people are in our neighborhoods right now like that slave girl, bound by the enemy in fear, depression, worry, sickness, loneliness? They are bound and yet we are free, with the keys in our pockets to unlock their torment. How long will we keep passing by for fear of the consequences of our involvement? We have so many excuses about why we can't get involved, but not one of them holds up when it is presented to God. Not our schedules, our inadequacies, or our abilities exclude us from our calling to this great involvement.

> God did not call us to a great invitation or a great suggestion; He calls us to a great involvement that realizes His greatest interventions.

Recently my husband went out to walk our dog on a nearby hillside. As he was walking, he came across an elderly gentleman who seemed distressed. As Steve was about to walk by, he felt God prompting him to stop. He knew from the man's appearance this stop would not be a short one. Aware of the many scheduled meetings that day, Steve was about to walk on. It was at this point the gentleman saw my husband and offered a greeting of good morning—and Steve got involved. What followed from that hello was a long conversation in which this gentleman shared some of his heartrending troubles. That led to them both going from the hillside to this man's home for coffee, where he accepted Christ and has since become one of our family's new friends, traveling with us to church and regularly meeting my husband for coffee. The encounter on the hill could have been avoided; but the decision rested with my husband's willingness to volunteer his time and attention to this unknown and unscheduled appointment. Our family made a new friend that day, and this encounter reminds us there is nothing more important than our call to be involved. This man's life has turned from hopeless to hope filled and from lost to found—but that turn began with a willingness to turn around.

CROSS THE ROAD

The parable of the good Samaritan gives us a great example of someone who knew how to get involved (Luke 10:25–37). When religion walked by and said, "I can't stop," the Samaritan saw a need and said, "I have to stop." Which would best describe your response: Are you more likely to say the reasons that you can't become involved or see the reasons that you can't ignore the need? The Samaritan ignored the fact he shouldn't stop; he didn't let prejudice or preferences prevent him from turning to help this wounded man. He chose to walk across the street, and in those few small steps he started the turn.

Walking across the street may not sound difficult, but it is often the thing we avoid the most. If we can just stay far enough away from the need, we can feel less responsible. If we can't see the full scale of the problem, we won't have to provide the answer. We can't turn a community around from the opposite side of our streets. Involvement walks across the road, knowing the cost that follows that crossing. The story goes on to show how the Samaritan's involvement moves from stopping to serving. He provides everything from bandages to transportation, accommodation to nourishment. The Samaritan didn't just offer the man a drink, because he knew water alone wasn't what this man needed. He didn't give him the number of a great hostel; he took him there himself and paid for this man's care.

> **Involvement walks across the road, knowing the cost that follows that crossing.**

This picture I find challenging as the good Samaritan demonstrates an involvement that speaks of such integrity. He doesn't do the bare minimum; he is diligent to take care of every detail. He commits to the process of this man's turnaround from roadside to full recovery. Our involvement needs to find the same level of integrity. God never underdelivers. When He crossed the street into your life and mine, He started a turn He intends to complete, from cleansing our sins to restoring our souls. He stays involved until He finishes the work He has begun (Philippians 1:6).

Yes, involvement means your dog walking may take an unexpected turn. It may mean you have people to pick up on your day out; it may mean stopping by the places you always just pass by; it may mean inviting people into your home before you expect them to go into God's home. In the busyness of all our lives, getting involved is a huge challenge. How do we have time to get involved? But if Jesus could find time to get everything done in only three years of ministry, then maybe some of the ways we spend our time need reassessing.

Someone needs you to stop today. Someone is waiting for you to help turn his life around. Someone is crying out for you to notice her. Someone needs God's intervention, and the key to unlock it is your involvement.

TWELVE

TURNING IT OVER

"WHERE DO I START?" MY SON ASKED AS HE EMPTIED THE entire contents of a jigsaw puzzle on the table. The sight of hundreds of pieces seemed overwhelming to him. From looking at the box lid this picture seemed an easy task to take on, but now faced with hundreds of tiny pieces his confidence began to dwindle and he was having second thoughts about the project he had embarked upon. I replied, "It won't take long; we can do it together," as I saw his enthusiasm dissipating quickly. "But there are so many pieces," he protested. "I know, but they all have a place. Let's start at the edges and work our way in," I answered. Reluctantly he agreed to come back to the table he had walked away from, and as I sat alongside him, we started turning each piece right side up as we began the process of making the scattered pieces resemble the masterpiece that the box lid assured us they made.

As we near the end of this book, maybe you, like my son, are more aware of all the scattered pieces around you than ever before. As your heart has taken in all the people and situations where God has positioned you to bring change, you can feel too overwhelmed to know where to start. The scale of brokenness or depths of division we are commissioned to turn around requires a consistent connection with the sustaining presence of God. It is His voice and spirit alone that will keep us engaged and involved when we feel like walking away. Just as I assured my son that we would achieve the task before us together, God reminds you as we close this book that He is in this process with you. He has committed to work with you until the work He began is completed (Philippians 1:6).

> God reminds you as we close this book
> that He is in this process with you.

THE CALL TO COMPLETION

God is a finisher; He doesn't walk away from the pieces others have left scattered. He doesn't get overwhelmed when the task seems too hard or the cost is too high. When He starts a turn-around, it is with the intention of making a complete turn. Every word God speaks He fulfills; every transformation He begins He completes. Therefore, when we are working with God we have to commit to the same process. We need to have the determination to keep going until we achieve the promised result. Maybe like my son with his puzzle you have started the process of putting things that were broken back together, but somewhere along the way you have lost sight of the end result. The vision of what God says you can achieve has been lost among all the overwhelming changes that have still to be made. We need to allow time for God to remind us once more of the box lid He holds for all our lives. We need to build into our turnaround process times when we go back to God's Word over our families, destinies, and dreams and see the picture God says is achievable so we can remain focused on the purpose of each piece we are handling.

At times, we can feel like we are making more mess than progress. Therefore, we need to apply daily disciplines that keep us focused on the task at hand. As my son became less interested in the puzzle, he would start to be careless, and then we would spend time searching for lost pieces or replace pieces put in the wrong space. Without regular encouragement and moments to refocus, my son would have left the table and the puzzle, never to return. The same is true in the turnaround process; we, too, have to find ways to encourage ourselves to keep going when we start to feel overwhelmed with the many pieces that are yet to find their place.

Unlike my son, we cannot allow ourselves to rely on others to keep us motivated all the time; there will be seasons in our turning when we may be isolated and uncertain of what to do. It is during those times we have to find the ability to stay strong so we can reach the promised results. Let's consider a few things that may strengthen you when you feel overwhelmed and encourage you to get back to the table where your turnaround awaits.

DON'T WORRY; PRAY

Someone once told me if you can worry then you can meditate, as worry is giving a lot of thought to what could go wrong rather than focusing on what you could do right. Taking control of what we give our time and attention to is a determining factor on how effectively we can bring changes to the world around us. Often we can take up so much of our time with things that may never happen and therefore leave less time for the things that we are called to put into action. Worry is a huge waste of time and potential, and we must tackle it before it terminates our turnarounds. We need to commit to taking every worry and replacing it with the power of prayer. If I can worry about tomorrow, then I can turn that around and pray for my tomorrow. If I am spending time worrying about my business, then I can replace that with prayer for my business. It may seem a simple idea, yet it is a huge battle we often fail to conquer in our minds.

> Worry is a huge waste of time and potential, and we must tackle it before it terminates our turnarounds.

The Bible says to put your mind on the things that are good and positive. Paul said, "Brothers and sisters, whatever is true, whatever is noble, whatever is right, whatever is pure, whatever is lovely, whatever is admirable—if anything is excellent or praiseworthy—think about such things" (Philippians 4:8). To bring change around us, we have to be able to change the thinking within ourselves. We have to turn around the negative mind-set and challenge those thoughts that try to turn us back from the progress we are making. When we venture into new areas, there will always be new concerns to navigate, but we cannot allow our worries to keep us away from the work we are called to take on.

In Luke 10, when Jesus was sending out His disciples to bring hope and healing to hurting lives, He told them to not take anything with them, no money or provisions. He sent them out to take on the challenge of reaching many in need when they were ill equipped to take care of their own basic needs. Jesus let His disciples know before they went that He would take care of their provisions as they took care of His purposes. He told them to go to homes in the places where they went and ask for food and lodging and if they were not welcomed not to stay and worry about how they were treated but to simply shake the dust off their feet and carry on. Jesus wanted to build within His disciples a tenacity that kept going and was more committed to the mission than worrying about the lack of provisions. If we don't turn away our worry, it will delay our progress.

Matthew 6:33 addresses the waste of worry by telling us to seek first the kingdom of God, and all the things we are worrying after will follow our seeking of Him. Worry only turns you inward, while prayer turns your thoughts upward toward your source. If worry is counseling you, it will take you out of the changes you are called to bring. I have wasted too much time worrying about what people think, worrying if people will support me and if the resources will come. While the worry was taking over my time and attention, I neglected the very places I was planted to bring change. Your turnaround requires your prayers and your meditation needs to be on God's Word, not the world's worry.

Your turnaround requires your prayers
and your meditation needs to be on
God's Word, not the world's worry.

FEED YOUR FAITH

Have you ever tried to open the lid on a jar and been unsure
which way to turn to loosen it? After several wrong turns you
end up with the lid closed tighter than it was when you started.
This is exactly how doubt works in our world; it is the tightening of a situation that God asked you to open. Doubt undoes
what we have already started. Just as progress is made in turning
something around, doubt can creep in and turn back what was
begun.

James 1:6–8 tells us that when we pray, we "must believe
and not doubt, because the one who doubts is like a wave of
the sea, blown and tossed by the wind. That person should
not expect to receive anything from the Lord. Such a person
is double-minded and unstable in all they do." Doubt is like
a man tossed about by the waves. In the turnaround process,
doubts are normal—there will be many times when what you
are endeavoring to do will cause you to question if it is worth it
or will succeed. Yet if we are going to see through our commitment to completion, then we need to be prepared for doubt's
arrival and plan in advance how we will answer. When doubt
comes knocking, we need to know how to send faith to the door
to answer.

| When doubt comes knocking, we need to know how to send faith to the door to answer.

Luke 24:13–35 relates the story of some disciples who allowed doubt to lead them away from where Jesus had asked them to wait for Him. After witnessing the crucifixion, their hopes of being reunited with Jesus were crushed. Though they had heard rumors of Jesus' resurrection and remembered His words assuring them of His return, they had seen Him killed. Doubt filled their hearts and began to cloud their judgment, so they headed in the opposite direction of where Jesus had asked them to stay. Doubt caused the disciples to go back to what was safe and comfortable when they were called to be Jesus' turnaround friends. As these disciples were now heading in the wrong direction, a disguised Jesus joined their conversation. He began to ask them why they had stopped believing and explained to them the reasons they should believe. As soon as Jesus left, they realized who He was. "Then their eyes were opened and they recognized him, and he disappeared from their sight. They asked each other, 'Were not our hearts burning within us while he talked with us on the road and opened the Scriptures to us?'"(vv. 31–32).

Doubt took them away from where they should have stayed. It placed fear in their spirits; but when Jesus entered their conversations, everything changed. Their spirits came alive and their hearts burned within them. When we are confronted with doubts, we need to lean into that same presence of the Holy Spirit; we need to allow His passion to melt the doubts and the conviction of His voice to silence our doubt. We must constantly remind ourselves of the instructions God gave us, and if there is a delay between the call and its fulfillment, then in that gap we must constantly feed our faith. Don't let doubt take you on a detour.

FUEL YOUR PASSION

Our passion will affect our progress in every area of life; how strongly we commit will affect how sacrificially we give of ourselves. When our passion is depleted, then so is the scale of change we can bring. Therefore, for our lives to achieve the maximum impact for God, we must know how to remain passionate about the things we have been called to do.

Caleb had served God wholeheartedly all his life, and his passion had seen him through many testing times. Caleb, alongside Joshua, was one of the spies who reported back about the potential of their promised land. When the Israelites refused to take their inheritance, Caleb tore his clothes and pleaded with the people to reconsider their choice. He watched a generation die from their lack of passion to pursue the promises of God. Many times on his journey Caleb had the opportunity to quit, to join the ranks of the noncommittal and the passive believers, yet his passion anchored him into God and he remained convinced that what God had said he would make happen would happen.

While others died never realizing their potential, Caleb was still holding on in his eighties. He declared, "Here I am today, eighty-five years old! I'm as strong as I was the day Moses sent me out. I'm as strong as ever in battle, whether coming or going. So give me this hill country that GOD promised me" (Joshua

14:10–12 MSG). His passion attained the prize as he stepped into the promised land and was given Hebron. Such was Caleb's passion that he did not allow time or age to weaken his will to see God's turnaround brought through to completion. His tenacity ensured he arrived in the place that God had promised. We must learn, like Caleb, how to feed our passion. We must not allow others' negativity to weaken our intensity.

Never apologize for your passion; don't let people calm down what God has stirred up. At several points I have allowed other people's comfort levels to determine my passion and conviction. I have concealed my zeal so as to not disturb their mediocrity, yet while I was concealing my desire I was also containing my destiny. I came to the realization that if I wanted to make my life count I had to be willing to let my passion lead the way. If you have lost your passion for the things of God, then commit to rediscover it—go back to your first love, to the joy of your salvation and to the power of His Word, and your passion for His purposes will be reignited. Without passion we have no fuel for our faith and our passivity can become the enemy's permission to live passively in the land that God sent you to turn around.

DIVINE INTERRUPTION

The truth is we can all feel like walking off the job God has assigned us to; for every triumph we may enjoy, there is also a trial we often endure. And our consistency in both triumphs and trials is what will ensure we keep the ground we have gained. God wants to remind us of His power in the places where we feel powerless. He wants to encourage every heart to stay on track. In Ezekiel we read a story where God does just that for His prophet. As we consider God's intervention to strengthen His prophet's involvement, I pray this would become your increasing reality of how your turnaround God is committed to help you at every part of your turn.

> **God wants to remind us of His power in the places where we feel powerless.**

In Ezekiel 37 we read that the prophet Ezekiel needed some divine intervention. He had served God faithfully, yet the people's response to God's Word was not as forthcoming. The people had come to Ezekiel to hear the message but treated it like a mere form of entertainment. Weary from the people's neglect of God's Word, Ezekiel became disillusioned. As his enthusiasm was waning, God came alongside him to remind him of all He was going to accomplish through His prophet.

As the prophet was on his way to deliver God's Word, God "grabbed" him (v. 1 MSG). I love the way *The Message* puts this, as often this is exactly what God's divine interruptions feel like. His interruptions are not gentle suggestions but radical ones, as God breaks through our weariness to remind us of our purpose. God grabbed Ezekiel and lifted him in the spirit to a place where he could gain a fresh perspective of his mission.

Often our weariness from our assignment to bring God's turnaround can affect our vision. Bringing restoration to the broken and hope to the hopeless can place a huge demand on our own lives before it asks for change from anyone else. Therefore we, like Ezekiel, need to know how to let God "grab" us.

FOR GOD OR WITH GOD

In our often overscheduled world, we can be so busy working *for* God that we stop working *with* God. At times when the weariness of the work seems overwhelming, we need to know how to let God interrupt our agendas. We may prefer God to lead us gently by the hand or nudge us slowly forward, but I have found when it comes to the areas where we are involved in the work of turning things around we are more often in need of an intervention that is more akin to Ezekiel's "God grab." If we do not allow God to grab us in these times of testing, then other things will. Things like fear, depression, and negativity will all happily take hold of our hearts; in the most vulnerable moments, they will remind us of the limitations we face and lie to us about our inability to remove them.

> In our often overscheduled world, we can be so busy working *for* God that we stop working *with* God.

Without God's grip on our lives, every turn we make will be in danger of being abandoned prematurely. We must endeavor to commit again not just to the work of turning but also to the relationship we have with our turnaround God. It is our ability to stay connected to God's eternal perspective that keeps our momentum in the moments where we face the most resistance.

Underneath my bed I have a long extension socket into which every night an array of devices are plugged in to charge. On several occasions I have returned to my devices in the morning only to find they are still drained of power. I have usually discovered the reason for the loss of power is that the main

213

socket that powers the extension cable has been pulled loose from the source. The same picture is what so often happens in our spiritual journey: the more we extend our lives to do, the more the drain on our lives. When we say yes to help restore the relationships or we agree to be a part of the answer in our communities, we are adding more demands and extension outlets to our lives. As a result it becomes increasingly important to keep checking that the plug from which all this is powered is firmly attached to the source. In every place where we involve, we need to also increase the checks on our connection to God; we need to match every growing demand with an increasing spiritual supply.

Our prayer life, the reading of God's Word, our worship, and our sacrifice are essential to our turnaround progress. If Ezekiel, who served God faithfully, needed a reconnection moment in his spirit, then we must ensure that we do the same.

WALK THE VALLEY

We often want God to lift us away from the things that make us tired and weary. Yet His refreshing is not to ignore the problem but to be reignited with a passion to bring the answer. When we are weary, maybe we need to ask ourselves how much we are working in our own strength and how much we are applying His spirit to the situation.

God followed this "grabbing" of Ezekiel by lifting up the prophet's spirit so He could then put him right back down in the midst of the needs he was sent to answer. So often we welcome God lifting us out of the challenges we face, but we are less willing for Him to choose the location where He sets us back down. Immaturity seeks spiritual escapism where maturity accepts responsibility. God was not looking to remove the burden from Ezekiel. This interruption was not to create a place of escape but to enlarge his understanding of what God was going to work with him to accomplish.

I have found in everything God calls us to do, He also enables us to do it. Though the work may be difficult, if God has assigned it, then He gives a grace that operates even in the most testing of times. He gives a peace that passes understanding, a peace that holds fast in the storms we encounter in this turnaround process. We cannot build a life where we look for the quickest exit at the hardest points; instead, we have to walk in the valley knowing the One we are walking in it with holds the directions for the way out.

| In everything God calls us to do, He also enables us to do it. |

One time, in Mark 4, Jesus told the disciples to take a boat to the other side of the lake—and during the journey the disciples encountered a storm. The disciples panicked as the waves hit the boat, but Jesus was sleeping. When they woke him, He questioned their faith and reminded them of His last instruction. He had set the coordinates for this journey: they were going to the other side of the lake, and if a storm happened along the way, that did not change Jesus' mind about the destination.

We, too, must learn in every storm to stay where our Savior sent us. We have to be able to see the job through, whether we are experiencing good or adverse conditions. Just because your business hits turbulence does not mean you should jump ship, and just because one relationship became bitter does not mean every other relationship will. We have to be willing to trust God, who is in our boat, and commit to get to the other side even if on the way we want to quit.

WHAT DO YOU SAY ABOUT WHAT YOU SEE?

After Ezekiel had walked his valley and seen the full scale of the dryness, God asked him a critical question: "Can these bones live?" (Ezekiel 37:3). God wanted to hear from Ezekiel's own heart where his faith was. He wanted to know if Ezekiel could visualize this valley of death being turned around to a place of life.

Each of us has to answer that question about the valleys in which we find ourselves. God knows the ultimate answer to this question. He knows He has the power to take the driest bone and bring it to life; but He wants you to know where you are in your faith in Him. He wants to challenge you in what you believe is possible.

As you have read the pages of this book, many questions may have been raised, but the most fundamental of them all is this: What do you say about what you are seeking to turn? If your valley is a relationship, He wants to know, *Can this relationship live?* If it is your business, He wants you to stand in that valley and answer His question, *Can this business be turned around?* God is asking each of us to examine what we truly believe, because our turnarounds will test our faith. Maybe you are not sure how to answer. Like Ezekiel, your response may be, "Sovereign LORD, you alone know" (v. 3).

What do you say about what you are seeking to turn?

Knowing Ezekiel was uncertain how to respond, God gave His prophet instructions of how to turn lifeless dry bones into a formidable army:

> Then he said to me, "Prophesy to these bones and say to them, 'Dry bones, hear the word of the LORD! This is what the Sovereign LORD says to these bones: I will make breath enter you, and you will come to life. I will attach tendons to you and make flesh come upon you and cover you with skin; I will put breath in you, and you will come to life. Then you will know that I am the LORD.'" (vv. 4–6)

TURNAROUND WORDS

Within this place of death God was about to bring forth life, and He was going to achieve this with the assistance of His prophet. God wants to do the same through you. Whatever valley you are facing, however dry the bones appear in your marriage, health, or business, God wants to work with you to bring His life. He sees an army where we see bones, and therefore we have to line up what we are saying with what God is seeing. God's instruction began with Ezekiel's confession; He wanted his words to become the seeds for this turnaround.

So often we can overlook the power we already have because we are more mindful of the death around us than the life within us. The Bible says, "The tongue has the power of life and death" (Proverbs 18:21). This is an incredible truth.

As Ezekiel faced dry, dead bones, God wanted him to revive them with the power within his own mouth. You may have heard this said before, but it is a truth we cannot afford to forget that there is a miracle in our own mouths. This is not a cliché, but it is a foundational truth that if we can master will hugely impact the changes we are seeking to bring. Maybe the way you are speaking about your situation is preventing it from turning. Ezekiel, who had become weary from the people's negativity, was being reminded to use his words to bring life. God was not instructing Ezekiel to ignore the problem, but He wanted His prophet to direct his words into the very place where the lack seemed most intimidating.

How often have our careless words lost us precious time as we have advanced in one moment but then lost the same ground with our own negative confessions? We have to harness the power of our tongues if we are going to make the turn.

My household is a blend of two nations, American and British. Over the years we have noticed some clear differences not just in our pronunciation of words but also in the way our differing cultures use words. Where my husband's American culture talks things up, my British culture talks the same things down. When London recently hosted the Olympics, this difference in our nations seemed even more apparent. My husband happily cheered on his Olympic hopefuls, but the British doubted their team's ability even before the games had begun. When we were chosen as the host nation for this great event, the immediate reaction from many across our nation was overwhelmingly critical. While some were overjoyed, others began to get very concerned about the potential problems the games could inflict on our town and cities. People complained of the inconvenience the Olympics would cause in their neighborhoods, the cost it would incur for the general public, and the pressure it would impose on our service industry. Then talk turned to our terrible medal history, our inability to measure up in the sporting arena. It was apparent that if we were going to see this event succeed, people would have to drastically change their confessions. This seemed an impossible task as the games were looming and many people had already become disengaged with this event.

Then something incredible happened as a brilliant idea began to be rolled out across Great Britain. Instead of the traditional torch-lighting ceremony, it was announced the torch would be carried across the length and breadth of Britain not by celebrities and officials but instead by citizens from each town who would be chosen from nominations sent in by friends and family in each community. This idea caused people in every community to speak up about the positives in the lives of those around them. They began to talk about those who were known in their communities for acts of kindness and service. Now those who had been passive commentators became potential torchbearers, and as this idea became a reality the mood of our nation began to change. As the flame went from town to town, larger and larger crowds started to turn up to represent their location and cheer people on.

That torch literally lit up our country; the ripple effect was huge as people up and down our country moved from indifference to involvement. That turnaround also was seen in our athletes, who now had the whole nation cheering them on. Athletes who had previously spoken cautiously of their chances of attaining a medal would talk as if the medal was already won, and as a result we ended the Olympics with the best medal board in British athletic history. Many things no doubt contributed to the successful hosting of the Olympic Games, but one huge factor that could not be ignored was the turnaround in people's conversations, and their affirmation became infectious.

Spiritually it is no different: we all need to align what we are speaking. Imagine if up and down your land everyone spoke with words that affirmed and encouraged the turnarounds we are called to make. We often have a mixed report, and therefore we end up with a mixed result. Do you remember in Numbers 13 when Moses sent out twelve spies to bring back a report on the land of Canaan, which was the Israelites' promised inheritance? When the reports came back from the spies, there was a conflict in their confession. While two spies spoke of the incredible potential they saw, the other ten had only a negative report— and with their words they were able to talk an entire generation out of their promise.

We have to become much more deliberate about our declarations. We must not let fear or insecurity take the microphone in our lives but allow God to strengthen our spirit so we can see death and yet speak life.

ACTIVATE THE ARMY

As Ezekiel obeyed and spoke, the parts of the body began to connect. Each individual piece started to move to become part of the whole; the bones found the tissue, the tissue found the sinew, and these random parts began to find purpose and function in their connection. Ezekiel stood alone in this valley of death, but an army of fighting men would soon join him. He had to have faith as a lone voice and call forth life. Ezekiel records this experience:

> I prophesied just as I'd been commanded. As I prophesied, there was a sound and, oh, rustling! The bones moved and came together, bone to bone. I kept watching. Sinews formed, then muscles on the bones, then skin stretched over them. But they had no breath in them.
>
> He said to me, "Prophesy to the breath. Prophesy, son of man. Tell the breath, 'God, the Master, says, Come from the four winds. Come, breath. Breathe on these slain bodies. Breathe life!'"
>
> So I prophesied, just as he commanded me. The breath entered them and they came alive! They stood up on their feet, a huge army. (Ezekiel 37:7–10 MSG)

We often ask God for the bones to attach before we will begin to act. There have been many times when I have felt discouraged by the lack of obvious support to what God has instructed me to do. I remember when I first announced I would be speaking at a women's meeting in my local church, my faltering announcement was met by an audible objection as three ladies shouted me down and left the room. I knew God had asked me to speak, but I was left asking, "Where is the support?" I wanted a bunch of cheerleaders, but instead I had to face a room full of dry bones. It is at this point we must find the persistence to press on, for as we do, things will begin to change.

God began to do what Ezekiel could not, and as the prophet

spoke God moved. God's moving started a movement between all the pieces that were scattered on the valley floor. He began to draw the disconnected parts together, and as a result the body began to be reformed. The bones and muscles rediscovered their purpose and increased their productivity as they began to move and find where they belonged. God's turnarounds are designed to achieve the same results within all our communities. There are many members of God's body who are yet to discover they have a part to play or a place to belong, and our words are to start the awakening of their purpose. We are to call to every disconnected piece to attach. Our turnaround mission may begin with a few, but it is destined to end with many more as each person reached is reunited with the Master's plan for his or her life.

God divinely interrupted Ezekiel's life to remind him once more of the puzzle box lid picture of all he was called to see happen. He showed him the army within the bones. God wants to grab your spirit to remind you again of the life He sees in your valleys.

My friend, as we now go our separate ways to outwork God's great turnaround, ask yourself again, "Where do I need to introduce God's turnaround power to my problem?" Is it a relationship, a business, a ministry, or a broken dream? Where have you said it is over too soon or there is no way where God can still make a way? This book is written to breathe belief back into your spirit, to lift your head, and to open your eyes again to possibilities that lay dormant in the places where you have turned away.

> Ask yourself again, "Where do I need to introduce God's turnaround power to my problem?"

God is ready, willing, and able to assist you in your turn. He is the God for whom nothing is impossible. So introduce your limitations to the God without limits. Dream a bigger dream for your neighborhoods, for the desolate and the broken. Re-enter your circumstances with a greater awareness of your ability to be the answer, and remind your spirit today that you serve a turnaround God and He is inviting you to take your turn!

> God is ready, willing, and able to assist you in your turn.

TURNAROUND PRAYER

Amazing God, I stand in awe of all You are.
You are Creator, Father, Friend, and my All-Sufficient One.
When You speak all creation responds.
You, oh Lord, are without limitation.
I pledge to You today my heart, my life, my all.
Use me to bring Your restoration.
Use my words to speak forth Your truth.
Use my hands to heal and my strength to serve.
Lord, You are my turnaround God.
I turn my heart to what breaks Yours.
I turn my ear to Your commands.
I believe that You can turn around my situation.
I believe that You can turn around my world.
I commit today to take my turn and play my part.
I am forever grateful to You, my turnaround God.
Amen.

ACKNOWLEDGMENTS

EVERY BOOK IS A TESTIMONY TO THE POWER OF FRIENDS AND family. And I want to thank some incredible people who have been a part of helping this book come to life.

First, to my amazing husband Steve and our beautiful children, Hope Cherish and Noah Brave: You are the greatest cheerleaders anyone could ever ask for. Thank you for your overwhelming love and never ending fun. You make me better!

To our awesome church, Life Church: To lead such a remarkable group of people is our greatest honor. You are servant-hearted and eternity-minded. Thank you for being those who demonstrate consistently to those in our community the love and power of our turnaround God. Our greatest days are ahead! Love you!

This journey of life is shaped by the company we keep, and I am so thankful for the incredible friendships God has entrusted to me. I want to say a heartfelt thank you to our dearest friends (you all know who you are)—your friendship is a constant source of joy that brings strength for the journey. Thank you for being you and letting me be me!

To the team at Thomas Nelson: Thank you for your commitment to this project, but more than that, your embracing of me into this family. Special thanks to Debbie Wickwire for her enthusiastic encouragement and belief in me. You have made this partnership a joy.

Finally, all thanks, honor, and glory goes back to God. He turned my life around and I will never be the same. He is my rock, my savior, my closest friend. I am completely in love with the one who is Love. I will forever serve the One who made Himself servant of all.